C000256479

Fabulae Classicae

30 Stories from

Classical Mythology

Fabulae Classicae

30 Stories from Classical Mythology

Christopher Beharrell & Stuart Padmore

Illustrations by Charles Harrison

Copyright © 2014 Christopher Beharrell and Stuart Padmore

Illustrations Copyright © 2014 Charles Harrison

All rights reserved. This book or any portion thereof may not be reproduced or used in any manner whatsoever without the express written permission of the publisher except for the use of brief quotations in a book review or scholarly journal.

First Printing: 2014

ISBN: 978-1-291-56230-9

Christopher Beharrell MA (Edin), Dip.Humanities (Open) was educated at Harrow School, St Andrews and Edinburgh Universities, and is currently the Classics Master at Woodcote House School, Windlesham.

Stuart Padmore MA (Oxon) has been Head of Classics at Lanesborough Preparatory School, Guildford, for 4 years. He previously read Literae Humaniores at Worcester College, Oxford, after being educated at The Manchester Grammar School.

Charles Harrison was born 1989 in West Lancashire and graduated in Graphic Design from Edinburgh Napier University. He now works as an Illustrator and Wildlife Artist.

This book is dedicated to the masters who taught me Classics at school, most of them now in Elysium.

C.B.

Fabulae Classicae – The Magic of Mythology.

The mythology of ancient Greece, adopted and adapted by the Romans, continues to fascinate us. Why?

First and foremost, the stories are full of imagination. Sometimes comic, sometimes heroic, often terrifying or tragic, they are like mirrors of human behaviour, which never changes; but they are given an extra dimension through the involvement of the ancient gods and goddesses in human affairs. The Immortals come down to Earth or up from the Ocean or the Underworld, in disguise or as themselves, to mingle with men and women in their struggles. Sometimes they act nobly but often, like humans themselves, they argue, sulk, take sides, make mischief, display petty jealousies and rivalries, and generally behave as badly as mortals.

When you add heroes, witches and monsters, the myths become even more fantastic and exciting; just look at Hercules, Odysseus, Jason, Bellerophon, Theseus and Perseus; the Hydra, Scylla and Charybdis, the Minotaur, the Gorgons, the Chimaera.

Most of the myths found in this book do not in fact deal with the great heroes or the monsters they fight, but they all involve gods or goddesses as well as human protagonists. The world of classical myth is also peopled with demi-gods, nymphs, dryads and strange creatures such as satyrs and centaurs.

In some of this book's myths, the gods reward mortals for showing the virtues of obedience, bravery, loyalty, perseverance or kindness; in others they punish them for disobedience, greed, ambition, arrogance or sheer stupidity. Many of the ones we have chosen were included in a book called *The Metamorphoses* by the Roman poet, Ovid - the word "metamorphosis" meaning "changing shape". In all his stories characters, whether gods or humans, change into different forms or shapes.

Above all, we today should read the Greek myths for enjoyment but, in so doing, we will also discover how they have influenced the ideas of writers and artists down the ages. Many of the greatest paintings in the world depict scenes taken from Greek mythology and, time and again, the characters of Greek mythology appear in poetry and prose; they also give their names to constellations of stars (Castor and Pollux), places on the planet (the Atlas Mountains) and expressions in our everyday language ("Achilles heel", "Herculean task") and so they continue to play a part in our lives today. We hope that all who make use of this book will be similarly touched by the magic of mythology…

C.B.

Fabulae Classicae – A foreword for teachers.

One major driving force which led us to assemble, in Latin, this collection of wonderful mythical stories was the feeling of need in the classroom for a multi-purpose resource, suitable for a range of pupils on different stages of their journey learning the Latin language. To try and meet this need, the stories which follow have been divided into four sections:

- CE Level 2 stories
- CE Level 3 stories
- 13+ Scholarship stories
- GCSE stories

Some of the thinking behind the creation of these four categories is now listed here, to allow best use to be made of them by teachers and pupils:

Length of the stories:

The stories in all four sections vary in length (partly because some tales need more words than others to do full justice to the fantastic mythical content). The stories in each section are not designed to be of the same length as the translation element of their corresponding examination, and rather should be viewed as practice stories of roughly the same standard but not necessarily length.

That said, in general the stories in each category are ordered in such a way that the shorter ones come first and the longer ones later in the grouping, to allow pupils to build confidence with shorter passages first.

Linguistic content of the stories:

Grammar and syntax – the stories in each section only contain examples of Latin grammar and syntax featured in the syllabus or syllabi relevant to that section according to the following breakdown (any grammatical or syntactical material outside the below will be glossed for pupils under the stories):

"CE Level 2 stories" and "CE Level 3 stories" reflect the prescription for these Latin examinations under the Independent Schools Examination Board (ISEB) Common Entrance syllabus for Classics.

"13+ Scholarship stories" **begin from, but go slightly beyond,** the listings of the ISEB Common Academic Scholarship at 13+ Latin syllabus. A small number of constructions (most notably result clauses and relative clauses expressing purpose) which do not appear on that syllabus do occasionally appear in this section of our collection. This is because such constructions were felt, upon investigation of many senior schools' unique scholarship papers (i.e. written by their individual Classics departments), to be commonly occurring and therefore worthy of inclusion.

"GCSE stories" reflect the common grammatical and syntactical ground of the following syllabi: OCR Latin GCSE, WJEC Level 2 Certificate, Cambridge Latin IGCSE. That is to say, any grammar and syntax which is not a shared feature of all of these will not appear. It is felt that teachers themselves can ensure that their pupils have met the remaining few features unique to their exam board's requirements in other full story contexts (e.g. gerundives of obligation for WJEC candidates).

NB: Where a verb has Classical precedent of multiple different constructions being used with them (e.g. being followed by a double accusative, by in + ablative or by the dative case), the one found to be most intuitive for the pupil, and with a Latin prose-author precedent, has been adopted.

Vocabulary:
Each section of stories has its own handy vocabulary index at the back of this book. Listed there will be any words not found on the relevant syllabus/syllabi as

above. The "GCSE stories" vocabulary index will list all words not common to all three of the syllabi referred to above.

NB: The vocabulary index for the "13+ Scholarship stories" **will not list and define any words which it is felt can be worked out by the pupil from an English derivative**. This is felt to be a scholarship level skill, and reflects reasoning employed by many senior schools when deciding which vocabulary to gloss on their Latin scholarship papers.

Questions attached to the stories:

Every story in this collection has a set of associated questions beneath it. This means that each of the 30 stories can be used by pupils in many ways: as a translation exercise, as a comprehension or grammar question practice exercise, or both.

The style of questions attached to a particular story has been designed to match the type of questions commonly asked on the relevant examination.
For example, the eight "CE Level 2 stories" and eight "CE Level 3 stories" have a mixture of comprehension questions and grammar questions of the various subtypes asked on those papers (derivation, changes to verb tense, changes to noun number, identification of parts of speech etc.)
NB: We have decided not to provide interlinear 'clue' Latin above CE-style comprehension questions – as has appeared on CE papers in recent years – as we feel this goes too far in 'spoon-feeding' pupils. Moreover, if by hunting more actively for the required Latin details to answer these comprehension questions in our collection, pupils are in this way being prepared to do more than they asked to at CE, then we view this as no bad thing.

Contextūs – We have felt that it would be negligent to create a collection of stories from Greek mythology without getting pupils to make some of the many connections they offer up naturally and constantly with areas outside them (such as with geography, religious studies, history, the natural world and more). To this end, many stories in the first three sections of the collection often have "*contextūs*" ("weavings together") attached to them, encouraging pupils to think about the content of the myth and 'weave it together' with other knowledge they may have.

NB: The "*contextūs*" found with the "13+ Scholarship stories" become slightly more sophisticated, both in their phraseology and in the scope of what they ask the pupil to do, often suggesting the type of independent study befitting of a scholarly approach. For this reason, these stories and associated questions are perfectly suited for scholars to do *after* they have sat their 13+ scholarship paper as post-scholarship work, just as much as for preparation before them.

Miscellaneous:

We have not used macrons on the Latin of all 30 stories, reflecting the convention adopted by the examinations relevant to each section.

The versions of proper names used for the characters from Greek mythology are almost exclusively the Roman names (where Greek and Roman names are different), since this is, after all, a collection of stories in the Latin language. All spellings/declensions of these proper names have been found to have Classical precedent. It is, of course, admitted that sometimes multiple Classical precedents exist for a given character, and under those circumstances we have tried to choose the version which candidates will most easily recognise the stem of in the oblique cases.

As teachers ourselves, we are often frustrated by pupils not recognising whether a proper noun is a person or place (when this is surely not the main obstacle we should want pupils to be focusing on). For that reason, as simplistic as it admittedly appears, we have decided to gloss all proper nouns on the same page beneath each story and to inform the pupil whether each word is a person or place in parentheses.

Also regarding the on-page glossing: we felt it is important to stoke pupils' intellectual curiosity with language, and so have occasionally included information in parentheses for pupils to ask their Latin teacher to explain to them if they are curious about a type of word more advanced than their syllabus - e.g. "(this is from a deponent verb)" sometimes appearing on glossed entries beneath the "CE Level 3 stories".

We hope all of the above helps to give a broad overview of how to make best use of this great collection of myths. nunc est legendum!

S.P.

CONTENTS

13+ SCHOLARSHIP STORIES:

GCSE STORIES:

Vocabulary:

LEVEL 2 STORIES

1. HERO AND LEANDER

The power of love soon puts Leander in a 'sea of troubles'...

Leander iuvenis erat. patria huius iuvenis erat Abydus, oppidum prope mare inter Asiam Europamque. trans hoc mare contra Abydum erat urbs Sesti, ubi virgo, sacerdos Veneris, Hero nomine, habitabat. Leander eam magnopere amabat et noctu trans angustias natabat quod eam convenire cupiebat. illa eum trans mare lucerna in turre duxit. olim tamen maxima tempestas orta est, et vis Leandri in undis altissimis deficere coepit. mox in aqua periit. undae corpus ad litus Sesti portaverunt. itaque postquam eum conspexit, Hero, tristissima, e turre in mare se deicere constituit. illa igitur quoque periit.

Leander, Leandri, m – Leander (a person)
Abydus, Abydi, f – Abydus (a place)
Asia, Asiae, f – Asia
Europa, Europae, f - Europe
Sestos, Sesti, f – Sestos (a place)
Venus, Veneris, f – The Goddess Venus (Greek name Aphrodite)
Hero, Herūs, f – Hero (a person)
noctu – "at night"
orta est – "(it) rose up"
vis, vis, f – strength, vigour (a noun, not a part of the irregular verb *volo*)
coepit – "(it) began"

Answer the following questions about the story of Hero and Leander:

1) Who was Leander and what was the name of his fatherland? (2)

2) Where was Leander's home city situated? (3)

3) Who was Hero? (3)

4) What did Leander have to do to meet Hero at night? (2)

5) What help did Hero give to Leander when he did this? (4)

6) Describe what happened to Leander in the very big storm. (3)

7) What did Hero decide to do after seeing what had happened to Leander? (3)

(20 marks)

2. PYGMALION

Pygmalion finds happiness after praying to the goddess of love.

Pygmalion vir Graecus et sculptor erat. statuas pulcherrimas faciebat sed tristis

erat quod uxorem non habebat. amicus ei dixit, "laetus esse debes! sunt multae

puellae pulchrae quas in matrimonium ducere potes. unam lege!" Pygmalion

respondit, "omnes aut superbae aut frigidae sunt. uxorem bonam numquam

inveniam."

olim Pygmalion statuam optimam puellae fecit. postea eam diu spectabat et

amabat. ille tamen flere solebat quod, ubi corpus tangebat, non vivum erat.

proximo die ad templum Veneris adiit et deam rogavit, "si tibi placet, da mihi

uxorem bonam!"

sculptor ad villam suam rediit et statuam conspexit. statua movit! puella viva

erat! Pygmalion, laetus, statim eam in matrimonium duxit.

Pygmalion, Pygmalionis, m – Pygmalion (a person)
quas – "whom"
in matrimonium duco, ducere, duxi, ductum – I marry
proximo die – "on the next day" (a phrase showing "time when")
Venus, Veneris, f – The Goddess Venus (Greek name Aphrodite)
quam – "which"

Answer the following questions about the story of Pygmalion:

1) Who was Pygmalion? (3)

2) What did Pygmalion make? (3)

3) Why was he sad? (2)

4) What advice did Pygmalion's friend give him? (4)

5) Why did Pygmalion think he would never find a good wife? (3)

6) What did Pygmalion then make? (2)

7) What did he then ask Venus to do for him? (3)

8) What happened when Pygmalion returned home from the temple? (3)

9) Explain why at the end Pygmalion came to live happily ever after. (2)

(25 marks)

3. DAEDALUS AND ICARUS

Daedalus' ingenuity cannot save his impulsive son.

Minos, rex insulae Cretae, vir malus erat. Daedalus inventor clarus erat. olim Daedalus cum filio Icaro ex Athenis ad Cretam fugit quod forte filium fratris ibi necaverat. Minos eum Labyrinthum aedificare iussit. deinde in hoc carcere monstrum terribile inclusit, nomine Minotaurum. corpus hominis caputque tauri habebat. postquam Daedalus Labyrinthum aedificavit, Minos eum Icarumque in turre altissima inclusit.

Daedalus tamen ingeniosus erat. consilium cepit. cotidie cibum avibus in fenestra posuit et tum pennas earum collegit. ceram quoque e nido apium in turre collegit. tandem, post multos menses, e pennis et cera quattuor alas fecerat. has alas sibi et Icaro adfixit et filium monuit, "prope me mane! ibi tutus eris".

e turre in caelum se iecerunt et, mirabile dictu, volabant! Icarus tamen audax erat et altissime volabat. sol ceram dissolvit et pennae dissiluerunt. Icarus in mare cecidit et periit. Daedalus, tristissimus, filium mortuum reliquit et ad Siciliam volavit.

Minos, Minois, m – Minos (a person)
Creta, Cretae, f – Crete (a place)
Daedalus, Daedali, m – Daedalus (a person)
Icarus, Icari, m – Icarus (a person)

Athenae, Athenarum, f pl – Athens (a place)
forte – (here means) "by accident"
Labyrinthus, Labyrinthi, m – The Labyrinth
Minotaurus, Minotauri, m – The Minotaur
consilium capio, capere, cepi, captum – I make a plan
mirabile dictu – "wonderful to relate" (this may be viewed as the opposite of the English phrase "sad to say").
Sicilia, Siciliae, f – Sicily (a place)

Below are 10 pairs of words – 1 word in each pair is a Latin word from the story above, 1 word is an English word which comes from it.

<u>Translate each Latin word and then explain the connection in meaning with the English word it is paired with:</u>

1) **insulae** and "insulation" (3)
2) **fugit** and "fugitive" (3)
3) **corpus** and "corpse" (3)
4) **collegit** and "collection" (3)
5) **multos** and "multiply" (3)
6) **audax** and "audacious" (3)
7) **mare** and "marine" (3)
8) **periit** and "perish" (3)
9) **mortuum** and "mortuary" (3)
10) **reliquit** and "relic" (3)

(30 marks)

* Contextus – Find the Icarian Sea on a map of Greece. Based on the story above, why do you think that stretch of water has that name?

4. PYRAMUS AND THISBE

A tragic tale which illustrates the danger of jumping to conclusions too quickly…

Pyramus et Thisbe vicini et amici erant. deinde amor eos tenebat. quamquam amore incensi erant, parentes eos convenire vetuerunt. rima forte erat in muro qui villas eorum dividebat. per hanc rimam Pyramus et Thisbe inter se dicere solebant. olim in silva media nocte convenire constituerunt. Thisbe ad hunc locum prima advenit.

subito leo ferocissimus appropinquavit. vultus leonis sanguine oblitus erat. Thisbe statim exclamavit et fugit, sed quod ea celeriter currebat, velamen in terram decidit. leo id violenter dilaniavit et sanguine oblinevit.

mox Pyramus in silva advenit, sed Thisben invenire non poterat. subito velamen dilaniatum conspexit. gladio se transfixit quod credidit Thisben mortuam esse. nunc Thisbe rediit et corpus Pyrami vidit. tum velamen et gladium conspexit et facta intellexit. illa igitur pectus suum eodem gladio transfixit et prope Pyramum periit.

Pyramus, i, m – Pyramus (a person)
Thisbe, Thisbes, f = Thisbe (a person - NB: the accusative singular of her name is "Thisben")
incensi – "inflamed", "set on fire"
qui – "which"
media nocte – "in the middle of the night" (a phrase expressing "time when")
vultus, vultus, m – face

oblitus – "smeared over"

dilaniatum – "torn up"

Thisben mortuam esse – "that Thisbe was dead"

facta, factorum, n pl – "the things that had happened"

eodem – "the same" (this word is in the ablative case)

Answer the following questions about the story of Pyramus and Thisbe:

1) What were Pyramus and Thisbe before they were lovers? (2)
2) How did Pyramus and Thisbe communicate with each other after falling in love? (4)
3) Why was it necessary for them to communicate in this way? (2)
4) When and where did the pair decide to meet? (2)
5) Describe Thisbe's reaction to seeing the blood-stained lion. (3)
6) What did Thisbe then leave behind accidentally? (1)
7) What did the lion do to this item that Thisbe had left behind? (4)
8) What two things did Pyramus do shortly after arriving on the scene when he was unable to find Thisbe? (2)
9) Why did he do the second of these two things? (1)
10) Describe what Thisbe did after she returned and realised what had happened. (4)

(25 marks)

5. PANDORA'S BOX

Pandora cannot resist temptation, with disastrous consequences.

Iuppiter, deus caeli terraeque, iratissimus erat quod homines mortales donum
ignis a Prometheo acceperant. eos igitur punire constituit. itaque dei puellam
pulchram, nomine Pandoram, fecerunt. Mercurius eam de caelo ad Epimetheum,
qui frater Promethei erat, duxit. "haec tibi uxor est", Epimetheo Mercurius dixit.

Iuppiter quoque Epimetheo arcam dedit. "arcam noli aperire!" inquit.
Epimetheus igitur arcam in villa sua celavit, sed Pandora eam invenit et clamavit,
"quid in arca est? eam aperi!" Epimetheus coniugi respondit, "Iuppiter me arcam
aperire vetavit." Pandora, irata, discessit et amicas suas visitavit. "fortasse
gemmae in arca sunt!" amicae clamaverunt, "O Pandora, arcam aperi!"

Pandora igitur ad villam rediit et, ubi Epimetheus non spectabat, arcam aperuit.
statim strepitus terribilis erat. Pandora perterrita erat. mala ex arca volaverunt: ira
et fames et morbus et mors, et multa alia, effugerunt.

Pandora arcam claudere cupiebat, sed nunc non poterat. tandem sola una parva
res supererat: spes! Pandora, misera, exclamavit, "nunc omnes homines mortales
illa mala pati debebit, sed spes semper aderit!"

Iuppiter, Iovis, m = The God Jupiter (Greek name Zeus)
Prometheus, Promethei, m – Prometheus (a Titan)
Pandora, Pandorae, f – Pandora (a person)
Mercurius, Mercurii, m – The God Mercury (Greek name Hermes)

Epimetheus, Epimethei, m – Epimetheus (a Titan)
qui = "who"
strepitus, strepitūs, m – a din, loud noise
res, rei, f – thing
spes, spei, f – hope
pati – "to suffer"

Below are 10 pairs of words – 1 word in each pair is a Latin word from the story above, 1 word is an English word which comes from it.

<u>**Translate each Latin word and then explain the connection in meaning with the English word it is paired with:**</u>

1)	**deus** and "deity"	(3)
2)	**terrae** and "terrain"	(3)
3)	**nomine** and "nominate"	(3)
4)	**frater** and "fraternal"	(3)
5)	**invenit** and "invention"	(3)
6)	**irata** and "irate"	(3)
7)	**clamaverunt** and "clamouring"	(3)
8)	**mala** and "malign"	(3)
9)	**spectabat** and "spectator"	(3)
10)	**mors** and "mortal"	(3)

(30 marks)

* **Contextus Primus** – Explain the connection between this story and the modern expression "to open a can of worms".

* **Contextus Secundus** – Can you think of the connection between the Latin word "arca" (found in the story above) and a holy 'box' in the Bible?

6. JUPITER AND IO

Jupiter tries to avoid feeling the effects of Juno's jealousy, with mixed results…

in urbe Argorum sacerdos deae Iunonis, nomine Ion, erat. Ion, nympha, ibi diu laetissima habitabat. olim tamen Iuppiter, rex deorum, eam conspexit et, quamquam uxorem suam habebat, statim amavit. mox igitur Iuno suspiciosa fiebat.

uno die, ubi maritus suus in agris cum Ione erat, Iuno de caelo descendere constituit. itaque Iuppiter magnopere timebat et Ionem in maximam vaccam mutavit. deinde, non iam perterritus, discessit.

Iuno tamen callidissima erat et coniugi non crediderat; Argum, qui centum oculos habebat, hanc vaccam custodire iussit.

Iuppiter, iratus, sine mora Mercurium ad Argum misit. nuntius deorum Argum necavit et Ionem liberavit. Iuno autem, quod a coniuge superari non cupiebat, asilum ad terram misit. hic vaccam momordit. Io igitur per totam orbem terrarum diu errabat. Iuno quoque centum oculos fidelis custodis Argi in caudam pavonis mutavit.

Argi, Argorum, m pl – Argos (a city in Greece)
Iuno, Iunonis, f – The Goddess Juno (Greek name Hera)
Ion, Ionis, f – Io (a nymph)
Iuppiter, Iovis, m – The God Jupiter (Greek name Zeus)
uno die – "One day" (a phrase showing "time when")
Argus, Argi, m – Argus (a Giant)

qui – "who…"
superari – (here means) "to be outdone"
orbis terrarum, orbis terrarum, m – The world

<u>From the story of Jupiter and Io above, identify and write down in Latin one example of each of the following parts of speech:</u>

1) A preposition followed by a noun in the ablative case.
2) A verb in the imperfect tense.
3) A verb in the perfect tense.
4) A superlative adjective.
5) A preposition followed by a noun in the accusative case.
6) An adverb.
7) A present infinitive.
8) A verb in the pluperfect tense.

(8 marks)

7. DIANA AND ACTAEON

Actaeon has an unfortunate end to a hunting expedition.

Actaeon, filius regis Cadmi, in montibus cum amicis venabatur. sol calebat et viri fessi erant. amici ad magnam silvam venerunt et dormiebant. Actaeon tamen, ubi per silvam ambulabat, parvam lacunam subito conspexit. ibi Diana, dea venatrix, nuda, se lavabat. ancillae suae exclamaverunt et ad dominam cucurrerunt. Diana rubuit, et irata in oculos Actaeonis aquam iniecit, quod sagittas suas invenire non poterat. "discede et dic amicis tuis quid videris!" Diana inquit.

Actaeon statim discessit et, laetus, intellegebat se celerrime currere. mox autem constitit et, imaginem in flumine spectans, vidit se cervum factum esse. "o, quam miser sum, quid faciam?" dixit.

subito canes sui eum conspexit et ad eum ruere coeperunt. amici canes hortati sunt. Actaeon dicere cupiebat, "ego Actaeon dominus tuus sum", sed verba ex ore non venerunt. deinde canes dominum ceperunt et, dum gemebat, dentibus lacerabant. Actaeon multis vulneribus periit.

Cadmus, Cadmi, m = Cadmus (a person)
venabatur = "(he) was hunting"
Diana, Dianae, f – The Goddess Diana (Greek name Artemis)
videris = "you have seen"
se celerrime currere = "that he was running very quickly"
spectans = "watching"
cervum factum esse = "had become a stag"
coeperunt = "they began"
hortati sunt = "(they) encouraged"

Using the story of Diana and Actaeon above, answer the grammatical questions below:

1) **montibus** - In which case is this noun? Why is this case used here? (2)

2) **oculos** - In which case is this noun? Why is this case used here? (2)

3) **iniecit** - Which word is the Latin subject of this verb? (1)
   Which word is the Latin object of this verb? (1)

4) **sagittas** – Change this noun to make it singular, keeping the case the same. (1)

5) **cupiebat** means "he was wanting". How would you say in Latin **"he is wanting"**? (1)

6) **sum** means "I am". How would you say in Latin "I was"? (1)

7) **verba** – Change this noun to make it singular, keeping the case the same. (1)

(10 marks)

8. ORPHEUS AND EURYDICE

Orpheus is given a chance to bring back his wife from the Underworld.

Orpheus filius dei Apollonis erat. olim Apollo ei lyram dedit. Orpheus optime canere et cantare poterat. ferae igitur e silvis ad eum veniebant et mollescebantur.

Eurydice nympha pulchra silvarum erat. eam Orpheus amabat et in matrimonium duxit. uno die illa per silvas errabat et satyrus, nomine Aristaeus, eam conspexit et persecutus est. Eurydice, perterrita, cucurrit, sed anguis eam in pede momordit. mortua decidit.

Orpheus tristissimus erat. itaque, quod uxorem petere cupiebat, ad terram mortuorum descendere constituit. ibi trans flumen Stygium transiit, et tandem ad solium Plutonis, regis Tartari, advenit. deum libertatem uxoris oravit, sed Pluto non audivit. regina tamen, nomine Proserpina, eum lyram canentem audiebat et delectabatur. illa coniugi persuasit. Pluto igitur Orpheo sic dixit, "uxorem tuam ad terram exteriorem tibi reducere permittam, sed dum ascendis respicere ad uxorem non debes."

Orpheus, laetissimus, statim discessit, et Eurydice eum secuta est. terram exteriorem paene advenerant, sed Orpheus ad Eurydicen respicere magnopere cupiebat. itaque, postquam eam conspexit, Eurydice statim in imaginem transmutata est et evanuit. Orpheus, miserrimus, iterum neque cantavit neque cecinit, sed in silvis cum feris habitabat. tandem multae feminae iratae, quod

Orpheus cantare non iam volebat, eum dilaniaverunt et in flumen partes corporis

lyramque iecerunt.

Orpheus, Orphei, m – Orpheus (a person)
Apollo, Apollinis, m – The God Apollo (his Greek name is also Apollo)
mollescebantur – "(they) were being softened", "(they) were tamed"
Eurydice, Eurydices, f – Eurydice (a person – NB: the accusative singular of her name is "Eurydicen")
in matrimonium duco, ducere, duxi, ductum – I marry
uno die – "one day" (a phrase showing "time when")
Aristaeus, Aristaei, m – Aristaeus (a satyr)
persecutus est – "(he) followed", "he pursued"
Stygius, a, um – Stygian ("to do with the Styx")
Pluto, Plutonis, m – The God Pluto (Greek name Hades)
Tartarus, Tartari, m – Tartarus (= the Underworld)
Proserpina, Proserpinae, f – The Goddess Proserpina (Greek name Persephone)
canentem = "playing" (accusative case, agreeing with *eum*)
delectabatur = "she was delighted", "she was charmed"
secuta est = "(she) followed"
transmutata est = "(she) was transformed"

Answer the following questions about the story of Orpheus and Eurydice:

1) Who was Orpheus? (2)

2) What was Orpheus able to do? (3)

3) Who was Eurydice? (2)

4) What happened one day when Eurydice was wandering through the woods? (5)

5) What did Orpheus decide to do as a result? (2)

6) Why did he decide to do this? (1)

7) What did Pluto tell Orpheus that he must not do? (3)

8) When Orpheus gave in to his desire to look back at Eurydice and caught sight of her, what happened to Eurydice? (3)

9) Describe what ultimately happened to Orpheus' body. (4)

(25 marks)

LEVEL 3 STORIES

1. PHILEMON AND BAUCIS

A husband and wife receive a reward for their hospitality.

olim in <u>Phrygia</u> in parva casa senex, nomine <u>Philemon</u>, et uxor, nomine <u>Baucis</u>,

habitabant. <u>Iuppiter</u>, rex deorum, cum filio <u>Mercurio</u>, ad terram <u>mutata veste</u>

advenit. nemo tamen eos accipiebat. tandem ad parvam casam advenerunt.

Baucis et Philemon eos libenter salutaverunt. cibum vinumque eis dederunt.

dum dei cenam consumunt, Baucis et Philemon vinum <u>se renovare</u> videbant.

deinde illi hospites cognoscebant et perterriti erant. "nolite timere!" dixit

Iuppiter, "hanc terram malam delebo quod homines mortales nobis amici non

fuerunt. e casa vestra discedite et nobiscum ad montem venite!"

ubi ad montem advenerunt, Iuppiter multam aquam in terram immisit. omnes

igitur perierunt. "propter hospitium vestrum vobis praemium dabimus," Iuppiter

inquit, "quid cupitis?" Baucis et Philemon deo responderunt, "custodes templi

tui esse et simul perire cupimus, quod semper laeti <u>una</u> viximus."

itaque Baucis et Philemon templum Iovis custodiebant et diu vivebant. subito in

duas arbores simul mutati sunt. hae arbores in loco eodem etiam manent.

Phrygia, Phrygiae, f = Phrygia (a country)
Philemon, Philemonis, m = Philemon (a person)
Baucis, Baucidis, f – Baucis (a person)

Iuppiter, Iovis, m – The God Jupiter (Greek name Zeus)
Mercurius, Mercurii, m – The God Mercury (Greek name Hermes)
mutata veste = "in disguise" (literally "with changed clothing")
se renovare = "was renewing itself"
una – (here means) "together"

Using the story of Philemon and Baucis above, answer the grammatical questions below:

1) **filio** - In which case is this noun? Why is this case used here? (2)
2) **eos** - What is the nominative masculine singular of this pronoun? (1)
3) **salutaverunt** - Which word is the Latin subject of this verb? (1)
   Which word is the Latin object of this verb? (1)
4) **fuerunt** - State the person and tense of this verb. What is the first person singular present tense form of this verb? (3)
5) **montem** – Change this noun to make it plural, keeping the case the same. (1)
6) **mutati sunt** means "they were changed". How would you say in Latin **"they had been changed"**? (1)

(10 marks)

* Contextus – The story of Philemon and Baucis might seem familiar to you, even if you have not come across it in Latin before. Can you think of where you have seen a related story, with similar content, elsewhere?

2. APOLLO AND DAPHNE

Cupid takes revenge on Apollo for insulting him.

olim deus Apollo Cupidinem iuvenem arcu et sagittis ludentem conspexit. Apollo risit et rogavit: "cur armis belli ludis, parve puer?" "arma tua occidere possunt. sed sagittae meae quoque potentes sunt", respondit Cupido. deinde, postquam haec verba dixit, sagittam auream in pectus Apollonis et sagittam plumbeam in pectus Daphnes iniecit. Daphne nympha, filia dei fluminis nomine Penei, erat.

ea viros non amabat, sed venatrix in silvis, similis Dianae, deae venationis, esse cupiebat. Apollo eam statim amavit et per silvas persecutus est, sed Daphne non solum deum non amabat sed etiam eum odisse movebatur. celeriter igitur fugit, magna voce clamans, "noli me tangere!".

Apollo, incensus amore, exclamavit "noli fugere! te amo. desiste!" ei appropinquabat et, ubi eam paene tangebat, Daphne patrem suum oravit ut se servaret. subito torpor gravis eam rapuit. corpus in librum, crines in frondes, membra in ramos, mutabantur. mox arbor facta est.

Apollo, quamquam tristis erat, nuntiavit: "haec arbor, nomine laurus, mihi sacra semper erit. victores ludorum et proeliorum frondes ex hac arbore praemia accipient.

Apollo, Apollonis, m – The God Apollo (his Greek name is also Apollo)
Cupido, Cupidinis, m – The God Cupid (son of Venus, Greek name Eros)
Daphne, Daphnes, f – Daphne (a nymph)
Peneus, Penei, m – Peneus (a God)
arcus, arcūs, m – a bow (this is a 4th declension noun)
persecutus est - "(he) followed", "he pursued" (the perfect tense of a deponent verb)
non solum…sed etiam – "not only…but even…"
odisse – "to hate" (this is the infinitive of a defective verb)
liber, libri, m – (here means) "bark (of a tree)".

Answer the following questions about the story of Apollo and Daphne:

1) What did Apollo see Cupid doing? (2)
2) What teasing question does Apollo ask Cupid? (4)
3) What is Cupid's response to this question? (5)
4) Describe where Cupid then fires his two different types of arrows. (4)
5) What did Daphne want to become? (3)
6) When she realises that Apollo is chasing her, what are Daphne's feelings towards the god? (3)
7) From whom does Daphne then seek help when Apollo has almost caught her? (1)
8) What transformation soon happens? (1)
9) Who, according to Apollo, will from this time on receive prizes in his name? (2)

(25 marks)

* Contextus – As well as victors in athletic contests, who else from antiquity do we often see depicted wearing laurel wreaths?

3. PROMETHEUS

Prometheus is punished for his disobedience

olim dei deaeque in Olympo habitabant, sed in terra nihil, nec animal nec homo, aderat. Iuppiter igitur imperavit Epimetheo ut animalia faceret. deinde fratrem illius, nomine Prometheum, homines creare iussit.

Prometheus lutum cepit et hoc in statuas virorum feminarumque formavit. tum statuis inspiravit ut viverent. postea omnes in terra laeti erant, sed Iuppiter ignem habere eis non permisit. Prometheus tristis erat quod homines frigidi erant et cibum crudum consumere debebant. itaque ad Olympum iter fecit et carbonem surripuit.

paulo post Iuppiter odorem coquendi in terra sensit. iratissimus ad Prometheum clamavit, "sceleste, cur mihi non paruisti? te puniam" itaque rex deorum Prometheum in monte vinxit. cotidie ex illo tempore aquila devolabat et iecur illius consumebat, sed id nocte iterum recrescebat. Prometheus, quod deus erat, perire non poterat. tandem post multos annos Iuppiter eum liberavit.

Olympus, Olympi, m – Olympus (the home of the gods)
Iuppiter, Iovis, m – The God Jupiter (Greek name Zeus)
Epimetheus, Epimethei, m – Epimetheus (a Titan)
Prometheus, Promethei, m – Prometheus (a Titan)
paulo post – "a little bit later"
coquendi – "of cooking"

Answer the following questions about the story of Prometheus:

1) In the beginning what was present on the earth?   (3)
2) What order did Jupiter give to Epimetheus?   (2)
3) What did he then order Prometheus to do?   (2)
4) After moulding the clay figures, what was the final step taken by Prometheus to carry out Jupiter's command?   (3)
5) What had Jupiter forbidden humans to have?   (1)
6) Why did this make Prometheus sad?   (4)
7) What did Prometheus therefore do?   (4)
8) What alerted Jupiter to what Prometheus had done?   (2)
9) Why does Jupiter say he is punishing Prometheus?   (1)
10) State three things that happened to Prometheus as punishment.

          (3)

(25 marks)

4. ACIS AND GALATEA

The Cyclops Polyphemus is moved to rage after his love is rejected, with tragic

consequences for others…

Galatea Nereis erat quae Acin, pulcherrimum pastorem iuvenem et filium

Naiadis, amabat. ille forte in Sicilia, insula Cyclopum, habitabat. omnes hi

Gigantes unum ingentem oculum in medio capite habebant.

olim Cyclops quidam, nomine Polyphemus, dum oves curat, Galateam in undis

ludentem conspexit et statim eam amabat. ei carmen cantabat, "O Galatea

carissima, pulchrior quam flores pulcherrimi, dulcior quam uvae, mollior plumis,

cur me fugis, crudelissima? ad me veni! filius dei Neptuni sum."

Galatea timebat et ad saxum in litore, ubi Acis sedebat, festinavit ut se celaret.

Polyphemus, tristissimus, in silvas erravit, sed subito respiciens illos conspexit.

itaque magna voce exclamans, partem e monte deripuit quam in eos iecit. Acin

percussit et occidit. deinde sanguis e saxo effundebat sed mox aqua fiebat. nam

dei Acin in flumen mutaverant. interea Galatea in undas effugerat unde postea

saepe rediit ut prope flumen sederet et Acin lugeret.

Galatea, Galateae, f – Galatea (a nymph)
Nereis, Nereidis, f – a Nereid (a sea nymph daughter of Nereus, a sea god)
Acis, Acis, m – Acis (a person – NB: the accusative singular of his name is
"Acin")
Naias, Naiadis, f – a Naiad (a water nymph)
Sicilia, Siciliae, f - Sicily
Cyclops, Cyclopis, m – a Cyclops (a particular race of giants)

Gigantes, Gigantum, m pl - giants
Polyphemus, Polyphemi, m – Polyphemus (an individual Cyclops)
Neptunus, Neptuni, m – The God Neptune (Greek name Poseidon)
fiebat – "(it) was becoming", "it became"

Answer the following questions about the story of Acis and Galatea:

1) Who was Acis? (4)
2) Where did Acis happen to be living? (2)
3) Describe the distinguishing physical feature of a Cyclops referred to in the story. (3)
4) What was Galatea doing when Polyphemus first caught sight of her? (2)
5) What three very flattering comparisons does Polyphemus make about Galatea in his song to her? (4)
6) Where does Galatea hurry to in response to Polyphemus' song? (3)
7) Why does she hurry there? (2)
8) How is Polyphemus described after Galatea hurries away from him? (2)
9) What actions does Polyphemus take which lead to Acis' death? (4)
10) Into what did the Gods ultimately transform Acis? (1)
11) After she had made her escape into the waves, why did Galatea often return? (3)

(30 marks)

5. CALLISTO

Jupiter is attracted to a mortal woman and his wife Juno reacts with anger and jealousy.

Callisto, femina pulcherrima, ab Iove amabatur. Iuno ei invidit et in ursam eam mutare constituit. Callisto, dum bracchia et crura nigris villis horrescebant, Iunonem oravit ut sibi ignosceret, "non mea culpa est quod coniunx tuus me amat." Iuno tamen non audivit. nunc Callisto, quamquam aspectum animalis saevi habebat, naturam humanam etiam retinebat. alia animalia timebat et eis appropinquare nolebat. noctu, in silvis manere timens, per terram errabat.

olim iuvenem venantem conspexit. statim intellexit illum filium suum, nomine Arcadem, esse. Callisto, laeta, ad illum ambulavit ut tangeret. Arcas tamen hastam sustulit sed iacturus subito inhibitus est. Iuppiter hastam corripuit et matrem filiumque in sidera mutavit. deinde eos in caelo inter stellas posuit.

Iuno, irata, ad Neptunum, deum maris, adiit et "noli accipere illam feminam filiumque in regnum tuum!" clamavit. itaque haec sidera, quae Ursa Maior et Ursa Minor appellantur, semper in caelo circumvectantur et, dissimiles aliis stellis, numquam in Oceanum descendunt.

Callisto, Callistūs, f – Callisto (a person)
Iuppiter, Iovis, m – The God Jupiter (Greek name Zeus)
Iuno, Iunonis, f – The Goddess Juno (Greek name Hera)

quod – (here means) "that", "in that"
aspectus, aspectūs, m – "the appearance" (a 4th declension noun)
noctu – "at night", "during the night"
venantem – "hunting" (this is the present participle of a deponent verb)
illum…esse – (here means) "that he was"
Arcas, Arcadis, m – Arcas (a person)
iacturus – "as he was about to hurl (it)" (this is a future active participle)
Neptunus, Neptuni, m – The God Neptune (Greek name Poseidon)
circumvectantur – "(they) ride around", "(they) are carried around" (this is a part of a deponent verb)
Oceanus, Oceani, m – Ocean (the great sea that encompasses the land)

Answer the following questions about the story of Callisto:

1) Who is Callisto?   (3)
2) What did Juno decide to do to Callisto?   (3)
3) What feeling towards Callisto prompted her to do this?   (1)
4) What did Callisto beg Juno to do?   (2)
5) What does Callisto say to Juno to try and avoid blame?   (3)
6) Describe Callisto's attitude towards other animals after her transformation.   (3)
7) Who is the young man that Callisto sees hunting?   (2)
8) Describe, in full, the action that Jupiter takes to avert disaster when Callisto and the hunter meet.   (5)
9) What command does Juno give to Neptune to get her revenge on Callisto?   (3)

(25 marks)

* Contextus – Can you think of any other constellations which have been so named because of events in tales from Greek mythology?

6. ARACHNE

Arachne pays the price for her pride and boastfulness…

Arachne puella Graeca et textrix clara erat. picturas pulcherrimas in tela texere poterat. superba tamen erat et de arte sua gloriari solebat. olim etiam dixit se esse meliorem textricem quam Minervam ipsam. Minerva haec verba audivit et Arachnen visitare constituit. ridens sed frigida, "picturas tuas videre magnopere cupio", inquit, "eas mihi ostende!" Minerva, postquam picturas Arachnes vidit, "hae optimae sunt", inquit. Arachne adroganter rogavit, "num texturae tuae non pulchriores sunt?" Minerva, iterum ridens, respondit, "ut illud decernamus necesse est nobis certamen habere".

itaque dea et puella multos dies texuerunt. tandem duae texturae finitae sunt. omnes qui in urbe habitabant venerunt ut eas viderent, sed Minerva statim intellexit opus Arachnes melius et pulchrius esse. iratissima dea texturam rapit et rupit. "quod tam pulchras texturas facis", clamavit, "in aeternum texes, sed nemo id quod texuisti cupiet." subito Minerva puellam tetigit et Arachne in parvum animal nigrum, octo cruribus et parvo capite, mutata est. non iam puella sed aranea erat, et ubique telas araneas in aeternum faciebat.

Arachne, Arachnes, f – Arachne (a person – NB: the accusative singular of her name is "Arachnen")
gloriari – "to boast" (an infinitive of a deponent verb)
Minerva, Minervae, f – The Goddess Minerva (Greek name Athene)

se esse – (here means) "that she was"
ut illud decernamus – "in order for us to decide that" (a present subjunctive is used in this purpose clause)
intellixit opus Arachnes…esse – "she realised that the work of Arachne was…"
in aeternum – "for all eternity"
animal, animalis, n – (here, in one of its rare uses, means) "creature", "insect"
telae araneae, telarum aranearum f pl – spider's webs

Below are 10 pairs of words – 1 word in each pair is a Latin word from the story above, 1 word is an English word which comes from it.

Translate each Latin word and then explain the connection in meaning with the English word it is paired with:

1)	**verba** and "verbal"	(3)
2)	**ridens** and "ridiculous"	(3)
3)	**ostende** and "ostentatious"	(3)
4)	**vidit** and "visual"	(3)
5)	**optimae** and "optimistic"	(3)
6)	**rogavit** and "interrogate"	(3)
7)	**iterum** and "reiterate"	(3)
8)	**duae** and "duel"	(3)
9)	**opus** and "operate"	(3)
10)	**facis** and "factory"	(3)

(30 marks)

* Contextus – The story of Arachne is a prime example of Greek myths often trying to explain features of the natural world around us. Can you think of any other Greek myths which do this? (Hint: Some other myths in this book also do this, but there are many more besides!)

7. KING MIDAS AND THE GOLDEN TOUCH

King Midas pays for his greed, but is forgiven in the end.

Silenus satyrus senex erat. corpus capri caputque hominis habebat. diu in montibus errabat et denique ad regiam regis <u>Midae</u> fessus advenit. Midas libenter ei cibum dedit et eum curabat.

Silenus comes <u>Bacchi</u>, dei vini, erat. Bacchus igitur, quod Midas comitem bene curaverat, praemium ei dare constituit. itaque statim discessit ut regem inveniret. mox eum conspexit et, "<u>quidlibet</u> tibi dabo" dixit. Midas celeriter respondit, "cupio omnia quae tango in aurum mutare."

"illud periculosum <u>esset</u>. num illud donum accipere cupis?" Bacchus rogavit.

"ita vero!" dixit Midas. "<u>ut libet</u>", respondit Bacchus antequam e regia festinavit.

Midas, qui nunc solus erat, circumspexit et tetigit mensam, quae statim in aurum mutata est. "vir divitissimus in toto <u>orbe terrarum</u> ero", exclamavit rex, qui circum <u>regiam</u> laetissime currebat et omnia tangebat ut in aurum ea <u>mutaret</u>. servis imperavit ut cibum sibi darent, sed hunc consumere non poterat quod in aurum quoque mutatus est. sic rex nihil consumere poterat! deinde Midas parvam filiam suam <u>amplexus est</u>, quae statua aurea statim facta est. "quid feci?" Midas miserrime inquit. tandem Bacchum rogare constituit ut se iuvaret. "te monui", Bacchus, subito apparens, clamavit, "sed cras in flumine te lavare debebis."

postridie Midas in aquam cucurrit. rex anxius, ubi ex aqua ambulabat, ripam tetigit. lutum mansit. postea, omnia in regia quae in aurum mutata erant, <u>solita</u> iterum erant. etiam filia Midae viva erat et patrem laetum salutavit.

Silenus, Sileni, m – Silenus (a satyr)
Midas, Midae, m – Midas (a king)
Bacchus, Bacchi, m – The God Bacchus (Greek name Dionysus)
quidlibet – "anything you like"
esset - "might be" (this verb is in the subjunctive mood)
ut libet – "as you please", "as you like"
orbis terrarum, orbis terrarum, m – "the world"
amplexus est – "(he) embraced" (this is the perfect tense of a deponent verb)
solitus, solita, solitum (an adjective) - as usual, as normal

From the story of King Midas above, identify and write down in Latin one example of each of the following clauses or parts of speech:

1) A relative clause.
2) A purpose clause.
3) An indirect command.
4) A question expecting the answer "no".
5) A preposition followed by a noun in the ablative case.
6) A preposition followed by a noun in the accusative case.
7) A superlative adjective.
8) A demonstrative pronoun.
9) A present participle.
10) A perfect passive verb.

(10 marks)

8. BELLEROPHON AND THE CHIMAERA

Bellerophon displays courage but proves the saying "Pride comes before a Fall."

Bellerophon iuvenis nobilis fortisque erat. in regia regis Protei habitabat, sed rex falso credidit Bellerophontem uxorem suam amare. itaque is iuvenem cum epistula misit ad regem Iobatem. in hac epistula rogabat illum ut Bellerophontem necaret. Iobates tamen, postquam epistulam legit, iuvenem necare nolebat quod iram deorum sentire non cupiebat. ei igitur dixit, "ex urbe mea discede, Chimaeram inveni et occide!"

Chimaera fera saeva erat quae caput leonis corpusque capri caudamque serpentis habebat. quoque ex ore ignem exhalabat. hoc monstrum terram populumque ubique vastabat. vates Polydus Bellerophontem monuit ut primo equum nomine Pegasum invenire deberet. Pegasus ex sanguine capitis Medusae natus erat. alas habebat et volare poterat.

Bellerophon nocte in templo Minervae dormivit. mox Minerva venit et frenum aureum ei dedit. postridie vir Pegasum in flumine bibentem invenit. equus ad Bellerophontem lente ambulavit ut ille in caput frenum imponeret et ascenderet. Pegasus cum Bellerophonte diu per caelum volabat, sed tandem Bellerophon

Chimaeram conspexit. eam una sagitta necavit et ad Iobatem rediit. rex laetissimus, "nunc tibi licet meam filiam in matrimonium ducere", inquit.

Bellerophon clarissimus erat sed superbus fiebat: credidit se deum esse. dei igitur eum punire constituerunt. dum vir in Pegaso equitat, Iuppiter asilum misit ut equum sub cauda morderet. Pegasus statim exsurrexit et Bellerophon ad terram iactus est. non tamen periit, sed ex illo tempore caecus erat, et ab hominibus vitatus est quod superbus fuerat.

Bellerophon, Bellerophontis, m – Bellerophon (a person)
Proteus, Protei, m – Proteus (King of the city of Tiryns)
Bellerophontem…amare – "that Bellerophon was in love with…"
Iobates, Iobatis, m – Iobates (a person)
Chimaera, Chimaerae, f – the Chimaera (a creature)
Polydus, Polydi, m – Polydus (a person)
Pegasus, Pegasi, m – Pegasus (a creature)
Medusa, Medusae, f – Medusa (a Gorgon)
natus erat – "(it) had been born" (this is the pluperfect tense of a deponent verb)
Minerva, Minervae, f – The Goddess Minerva (Greek name Athene)
tibi licet – "it is allowed for you" (this is an example of an impersonal verb)
in matrimonium duco, ducere, duxi, ductum – I marry
Iuppiter, Iovis, m – The God Jupiter (Greek name Zeus)
se…esse – "that he was…"

Below are 10 pairs of words – 1 word in each pair is a Latin word from the story above, 1 word is an English word which comes from it.

<u>Translate each Latin word and then explain the connection in meaning with the English word it is paired with:</u>

1)	**iuvenis** and "juvenile"	(3)
2)	**habitabat** and "habitation"	(3)
3)	**credidit** and "credible"	(3)
4)	**legit** and "legible"	(3)
5)	**urbe** and "urban"	(3)
6)	**deberet** and "debt"	(3)
7)	**dormivit** and "dormitory"	(3)
8)	**ambulavit** and "amble"	(3)
9)	**superbus** and "superb"	(3)
10)	**constituerunt** and "constitution"	(3)

(30 marks)

13+ SCHOLARSHIP STORIES

1. VENUS AND ADONIS

Venus is made to fall in love with the handsome mortal Adonis, setting a tragic chain of events in motion…

olim <u>Venus</u> cum filio <u>Cupidine</u> in agris ludebat. ille matrem sagitta forte vulneravit. deinde dea iuvenem pulchrum, nomine <u>Adonidem</u>, vidit et statim amabat. Adonis venator erat et in silvis multa animalia - ursos luposque leonesque - petere solebat. Venus tamen eum monuit: "noli persequi animalia saevissima quod te aut vulnerare aut occidere possunt." sed Adonis, qui audax et superbus erat, risit et ei dixit: "nec leones nec ursos nec ulla animalia timeo." tum vir Veneri promisit dentem apri <u>se relaturum esse</u>.

is hastam et arcum sustulit, et in silvas festinavit ut aprum peteret. mox, maximo apro conspecto, hasta feram <u>vulneraturus</u> erat. subito tamen aper, ad Adonidem ruens, dentibus longis eum oppugnavit. Venus, quae in curru per caelum movebat, strepitum audivit et quam celerrime descendit ut amantem servaret. sed mortuus est. tristissima, Venus sanguinem Adonidis in rubras <u>anemonas</u>, quae quotannis reviviscunt, mutavit.

Venus, Veneris, f – The Goddess Venus (Greek name Aphrodite)
Cupido, Cupidinis, m – The God Cupid (Greek name Eros)
Adonis, Adonidis, m – Adonis (a person)
se relaturum esse – "that he would bring back" (there is a future active infinitive in the indirect statement here)
vulneraturus – "(being) about to wound" (this is a future active participle)

anemone, anemones, f – "anemone" or "windflower" (NB: this noun declines in an unusual way, mixing some Greek endings with some endings from Latin's 1ˢᵗ declension)

Answer the following questions about the story of Venus and Adonis:

1) What was Venus doing at the outset of this story? (3)
2) Describe what happened to Venus after she was accidentally wounded by one of Cupid's arrows. (4)
3) What warning did Venus give to the hunter Adonis? (3)
4) What reason did Venus give Adonis for her warning? (3)
5) What two personality traits led Adonis to ignore Venus' warning? (2)
6) Describe, in full, the actions suddenly taken by the wild boar as Adonis was about to wound it with his spear. (5)
7) What action did Venus take after hearing the din below? (2)
8) What was her purpose in taking this action? (2)
9) Describe, in full, the action taken by the grief-stricken Venus at the end of this sad tale to honour the memory of her lost lover? (6)

(30 marks)

* **Contextus Fabulae– This story involves Adonis, the mortal favourite of Venus (Aphrodite), meeting a tragic end. A similar fate befalls Hippolytus, the mortal favourite of Diana (Artemis). Do some independent research to find out what happens to Hippolytus!**

* **Contextus Linguae– This story includes examples of a future active participle and a future active infinitive. Talk to your teacher about how these are formed in Latin (perhaps you already have an idea yourself after seeing the examples in the story!).**

2. JUPITER AND GANYMEDE

The King of the Gods, Jupiter, wants to take the handsome young mortal, Ganymede, to be cupbearer to the Gods on Mount Olympus. This sets a chain of events in progress for the later creation of two new astrological constellations…

olim prope urbem Troiae, in monte Ida, iuvenis pulcherrimus, oves curans ambulabat. hic iuvenis, nomine Ganymedes, a Iove spectabatur. rex deorum exclamavit: "puerum pulchriorem numquam vidi! mihi placet eum ad caelum auferre. sine dubio pincerna optimus deis erit." Iuppiter igitur aquilam suam emittere constituit ut iuvenem quam celerrime caperet.

cum aquila Ganymedem in caelum abstulisset, Iuppiter puero dona immortalitatis et primae aetatis aeternalis dedit. omnes dei Ganymedem amabant – Iuno sola puerum non amabat. itaque Iuppiter, ut iram uxoris molliret, cum Ganymedes pincerna deorum diu fuisset, eum inter stellas posuit: nunc hic iuvenis pulcherrimus sidus nomine Aquarius factus est. Iuppiter quoque aquilam, quae puerum abstulerat, sidus nomine Aquilam fecit.

Troia, Troiae, f – Troy (a place)
Ida, Idae, f – Ida (the name of a mountain)
Ganymedes, Ganymedis, m – Ganymede (a young Trojan prince at a time long before the Trojan War).
Iuppiter, Iovis, m – The God Jupiter (Greek name Zeus)
pincerna, pincernae, m – cupbearer (NB: This is one of the unusual **masculine** 1st declension nouns)
Iuno, Iunonis, f – The Goddess Juno (Greek name Hera)

Answer the following questions about the story of Jupiter and Ganymede:

1) What was the very handsome young man doing on Mount Ida at the outset of the story? (2)

2) What action does Jupiter claim it will please him to take regarding Ganymede? (2)

3) What does Jupiter say tgar Ganymede will turn out to be? (3)

4) Describe, in full, what action Jupiter therefore decides to take and for what purpose he does this. (5)

5) What two gifts does Jupiter then bestow upon Ganymede? (2)

6) After Ganymede had been cupbearer to the gods for a long time, what action did Jupiter take? (2)

7) Why did he take this action? (3)

8) Describe, in full, the two transformations that Jupiter brings about at the end of the story to honour two of its characters. (6)

(25 marks)

* **Contextus Fabulae–** This story involves extraordinary events unfolding around a shepherd (Ganymede) on Mount Ida. Can you think of another famous Greek mythical story where a different young man, minding his own business on Mount Ida, has his life similarly turned upside down by the intervention of the Gods?

* **Contextus Fabulae–** Do some independent research to determine what the astronomical connection is in our solar system between Jupiter and Ganymede. Can you see how that connection ties in with the content of the above story?

* **Contextus Linguae–** The Latin noun "pincerna" ("cupbearer") is a rare example of a Latin noun that belongs to the 1st declension but is masculine (not feminine). List as many other such nouns as you can think of – hint: think of male jobs to help you get started!

3. SATURN AND THE GOLDEN AGE

The God Saturn, having fled from Mount Olympus, brings civilisation and a "Golden Age" to Italy.

olim <u>Saturnus</u>, a filio suo <u>Iove</u> e monte <u>Olympo</u> expulsus, ad <u>Italiam</u> advenit. ille incolas Italiae composuit et eis leges dedit. Saturnus quoque illum locum "<u>Latium</u>" vocari maluit, quod ipse, arma Iovis fugiens, tutus ibi latuerat. mox rex Latii factus est, et populum artes agriculturae docuit. suum populum in tale placida pace regebat ut homines haec saecula "aurea" appellarent.

paulatim tamen rabies belli et amor rerum in hoc loco orti sunt: homines peiora metalla invenerunt, et cum ferrum invenissent, hoc gladios mox faciebant. quibus visis, Saturnus lacrimavit et ex Italia exiit.

Romani autem postea in saeculis aureis Saturni diu gaudebant. festum nomine "<u>Saturnalia</u>" conviviis agebant, ubi servi unum diem liberi erant et domini eorum servi facti sunt.

Saturnus, Saturni, m – The God Saturn (associated by the Romans with the Greek God "Cronus")
Iuppiter, Iovis, m – The God Jupiter (Greek name Zeus)
Olympus, Olympi, m – Olympus (the home of the Gods)
Italia, Italiae, f – Italy
Latium, Latii, n – Latium (the name of a place)
Saturnalia, Saturnalium, n pl – The Saturnalia (a festival held by the Romans)

Answer the following questions about the story of Saturn and the Golden Age:

1) What drove Saturn to go to Italy? (3)
2) In what two ways did Saturn help the locals after he arrived in Italy? (2)
3) Explain, with reference to a Latin word in the story, why Saturn wanted the place to be named "Latium". (4)
4) What further help did Saturn give to his people after he had been made king? (2)
5) What about Saturn's reign meant that people called it "the Golden Age"? (2)
6) The rise of which two feelings in his realm started the disruption of Saturn's "Golden Age"? (2)
7) The discovery of which metal in particular further disrupted the "Golden Age"? (1)
8) What did men learn to do with this metal? (2)
9) Describe the actions taken by Saturn after he witnessed this degeneration in his realm. (3)
10) Describe, in full, the custom adopted by Roman slaves and their masters at banquets of the Saturnalia festival to commemorate Saturn's "Golden Age". (4)

(25 marks)

* Contextus Fabulae– This story explains the origins of the Roman "Saturnalia" festival. Do some further exploration into this festival – When was it held? What special clothing was worn by some of the participants? Etc.

* Contextus Fabulae– The content of this story is influenced by a small number of lines from Vergil's *Aeneid*. If you are interested in reading the original lines about Saturn's Golden Age written by the Roman poet Vergil, ask your teacher to start you off translating *Aeneid* Book 8 lines 320-330.

4. MERCURY, JUTURNA AND LARA

Jupiter takes a fancy to a beautiful river Goddess, called Juturna, and punishes one of her sisters, Lara, for helping Juturna escape him. Mercury then wickedly takes advantage of the nature of that punishment…

olim Iuppiter deam, nomine Iuturnam, magnopere amabat. illa aut in silvis aut in fluminibus totiens latebat ut Iuppiter iratissimus esset. ille, igitur, omnes nymphas convocare constituit: "soror vestra, Iuturna, sibi auxilio non est," inquit, "concumbere maximo deo Iuturnae bono erit. vos eam in flumine latere conantem capite!" his verbis dictis, omnes nymphae adnuerunt.

sed, cum Iuturna ad flumen accurrisset, una nympha, Lara nomine, sorori (et quoque Iunoni) omnia, quae Iuppiter locutus erat, patefecit. Iuppiter linguam Larae iratissime eripuit et, Mercurio ad se vocato, dixit: "in Tartarum eam duc!" Mercurius domino paruit et Laram ad Tartarum ducebat. in itinere tamen nymphae pulchrae concumbere volebat, et quod vocem non iam habebat, misera Lara denegare non poterat. mox gemini, Lares nomine, nati sunt.

Iuppiter, Iovis, m – The God Jupiter (Greek name Zeus)
Iuturna, Iuturnae, f – Juturna (a Goddess)
auxilio non est – (literally means) "is not being a source of help"
Iuturnae bono erit – (literally means) "(it) will be a source of advantage for" Juturna
Lara, Larae, f – Lara (a nymph)
Iuno, Iunonis, f – Juno (Queen of the Gods, Wife of Jupiter)
Mercurius, Mercurii, m – The God Mercury (Greek name Hermes)
Tartarus, Tartari, m – Tartarus (a name for the Underworld)
Lares, Larum, m pl – The "Lares" (deities in Roman religion)

Answer the following questions about the story of Mercury, Juturna and Lara:

1) What was Juturna doing so often that she angered Jupiter? (3)
2) What does the enraged Jupiter therefore decide to do?   (2)
3) What (precise) command relating to Juturna does Jupiter give the other nymphs?   (4)
4) How do the nymphs react when given this command?   (2)
5) How does Lara then disobey Jupiter and aid the causes of both Juturna and Juno?   (4)
6) At the height of his anger, what physical punishment does Jupiter inflict upon Lara?   (2)
7) What command, designed to further punish Lara, does Jupiter then give to Mercury?   (2)
8) What hidden agenda did Mercury have on the journey?   (3)
9) Explain why Lara is unable to stop Mercury from getting his wish.   (3)

(25 marks)

* **Contextus Fabulae– This mythical story tries to explain the origin of an important feature of Roman religion – the Lares. Make a short summary of what role the Lares played in ancient Roman religion (hint: you may already know what a "lararium" was in a Roman villa!).**

* **Contextus Linguae– This story contains two examples (both glossed for you) of an unusual use of the dative case in Latin. Ask your teacher about, or do some research of your own into, what Latin's "predicative dative" looks like and how we translate it.**

5. MARS, VENUS AND VULCAN

The War God Mars cannot resist the beauty of Venus, Goddess of Love, but

ultimately is foiled by her husband Vulcan.

olim, <u>Mars</u>, deus belli, <u>Venerem</u> per agros ambulantem conspexit. ille eam statim amavit et, quamquam Venus <u>Volcanum</u> coniugem habebat, deae pulcherrimae concumbere magnopere cupiebat. Mars igitur, cum Volcanus a regia sua abesset, Venerem visitare solebat ut ei dona daret. mox clam <u>amantes</u> fiebant. <u>Sol</u> tamen amplexus illorum viderat, et sine mora amicum Volcanum <u>certiorem fecit</u>.

Volcanus tam iratus erat ut Venerem et Martem ulcisci constitueret. itaque, ut duos deos improbos caperet, rete ingens, quod videri non poterat, fecit. Volcanus hoc rete circum lectum finxit. uno die Mars, amore inflammatus, iterum in hunc lectum cum Venere iniit. capti in insidiis Volcani movere non poterant. deus claudus revenit et, exsultans, omnes alios deos ad suam regiam vocavit ut spectaculum viderent et Martem victum deriderent.

cum denique Volcanus amantes liberavisset, Mars, pudore motus, maximum aurum et plurima dona Volcano dedit.

Mars, Martis, m – The God Mars (Greek name Ares)
Venus, Veneris, f – The Goddess Venus (Greek name Aphrodite)
Volcanus, Volcani, m – The God Vulcan, (God of fire and blacksmiths, Greek name Hephaestus)
amans, amantis, m/f - a lover
Sol, Solis, m – The Sun (a God)
certiorem facio, facere, feci, factum – I make someone more certain (i.e. "inform" them)

Below are 10 Latin words from the story above. For each one:

a) Translate the Latin word

b) Think of an English word which you believe has come from the Latin word – don't be afraid to use an English dictionary to help you if necessary!

c) Explain the connection in meaning between the Latin word and your chosen English derivative:

E.g. motus = "(having been) moved" – gives us the English word "motion", with the connection being that motion means "movement".

1)	belli	(3)
2)	coniugem	(3)
3)	dona	(3)
4)	Sol	(3)
5)	inflammatus	(3)
6)	capti	(3)
7)	insidiis	(3)
8)	exsultans	(3)
9)	omnes	(3)
10)	deriderent	(3)

(30 marks)

* Contextus Fabulae– This mythical story is told (using the Greek counterparts to the Roman deities in the story above) by the Greek epic poet Homer in his *Odyssey* (Book 8 Lines 256ff). Find out where Odysseus has reached on his epic journey home when this story is told by the bard Demodocus – Which race of people is he staying with? Who is the King of that people? How close to getting home is Odysseus at this stage of his adventures?

(If you find that research interesting, consider reading the Odyssey in translation in full if you have not already done so – it is one of the world's greatest pieces of literature!)

6. NEPTUNE AND MINERVA

The God Neptune takes on the Goddess Minerva in a contest to determine who
will become patron God(dess) of a new Greek city...

olim deus <u>Neptunus</u> et dea <u>Minerva</u> (quae a Graecis Athene appellabatur) certamen habebant quod custos urbis novae et pulcherrimae esse volebant. rex huius urbis, nomine <u>Cecrops</u>, rogare deos constituerat ut populo urbis dona darent. Neptunus, primum, terram tam vehementer tridente pulsavit ut fons statim ad caelum ortus est.

primo cives urbis laeti erant, quod putabant fontem multam aquam sibi <u>paraturum esse</u>. mox tamen, cum cives fonti appropinquavissent, irati facti sunt quod invenerunt aquam salsam esse et igitur se non posse eam bibere.

deinde Minerva donum suum populo dedit: in terram unam minimam olivam imposuit. cives nunc laetissimi erant quod ex his arboribus cibum et materiam oleumque obtinere poterant.

Cecrops igitur, sine mora, adfirmavit Minervam victricem esse.

Neptunus tam iratus erat ut maximum <u>flumen</u> ad urbem emitteret et, victus, in undas maris iterum reveniret.

Neptunus, Neptuni, m – The God Neptune (Greek name Poseidon)
Minerva, Minervae, f – The Goddess Minerva (Greek name Athene)
Cecrops, Cecropis, m – Cecrops (an unusual early King of Athens who was half man and half snake)
paraturum esse – "would provide" (this is a future active infinitive)
flumen, fluminis, n – (here means) "a flood"

Below are 10 Latin words from the story above. For each one:

a) **Translate the Latin word**

b) **Think of an English word which you believe has come from the Latin word – don't be afraid to use an English dictionary to help you if necessary!**

c) **Explain the connection in meaning between the Latin word and your chosen English derivative:**

E.g. maris = "of the sea" – gives us the English word "marine", with the connection being that marine animals live in the sea.

1)	custos	(3)
2)	volebant	(3)
3)	vehementer	(3)
4)	cives	(3)
5)	posse	(3)
6)	imposuit	(3)
7)	arboribus	(3)
8)	flumen	(3)
9)	emitteret	(3)
10)	undas	(3)

(30 marks)

* Contextus Fabulae– This mythical story explains why the city of Athens came to be called "Athens". Other cities in the Greek and Roman world can have their names traced back to individual Gods or mortals too. Do some detective work to discover the connection in names between the following pairs:

a) An ancient Roman town, destroyed (but also preserved) by volcanic pyroclastic flows in AD79 and a famous mythical demi-God.

b) A strategically-important sea port in Roman Egypt and a famous king of Macedon.

c) The city of Abdera in Greece and a character in one of the Twelve Labours of Hercules.

7. PLUTO, JUPITER AND NEPTUNE

The God Pluto and his two brothers decide how they will split the world up between them in order to rule it…

iampridem, cum dei <u>Olympiani</u>, <u>Iove</u> ducente, <u>Titanes</u> superavissent, deus <u>Pluto</u> et duo fratres, <u>Neptunus</u> et Iuppiter, <u>orbem terrarum</u> inter se dividere volebant. itaque tres partes orbis terrarum creare constituerunt. hae partes caelum et mare et <u>Tartarus</u> erant.

omnes fratres caelum obtinere magnopere volebant. mox igitur putabant, ut rem iuste decernerent, optimum <u>futurum esse</u> sortiri. postquam Iuppiter regnum caeli sic accepit et Neptunus dominus maris factus est, Pluto sortem Tartari obtinuit.

his constitutis, Pluto <u>triste</u> ad Tartarum iter fecit ut rex mortuorum esset. ibi ille tres iudices animarum mortuorum designavit. hi, qui filii mortales Iovis fuerant, Rhadamanthus, Aeacus et Minos appellabantur. Pluto quoque uxorem, nomine Proserpinam, dolo cepit, sed illa alia fabula est…

Olympianus, a, um – Olympian
Iuppiter, Iovis, m – The God Jupiter (Greek name Zeus)
Titan, Titanis, m – a Titan
Pluto, Plutonis, m – The God Pluto (Greek name Hades)
Neptunus, Neptuni, m – The God Neptune (Greek name Poseidon)
orbis terrarum, orbis terrarum, m – The world
Tartarus, Tartari, m – Tartarus (a name for The Underworld)
futurum esse = "it would be" (this is the future active infinitive of *sum, esse, fui*)
triste – sadly (an adverb)

From the story of Pluto, Jupiter and Neptune above, answer the following questions relating to types of clauses found in the Latin:

1) Identify and write down a relative clause.
2) Identify and write down an ablative absolute.
3) Identify and write down a cum clause (i.e. a temporal clause using a subjunctive).
4) Explain why **esset** is in the subjunctive mood.

From the story of Pluto, Jupiter and Neptune above, identify and write down in Latin one example of each of the following parts of speech:

5) A cardinal number.
6) An imperfect passive verb.
7) A reflexive pronoun.
8) A demonstrative pronoun.
9) An irregular superlative adjective.
10) An infinitive from a deponent verb.

Change the following words from the above story in the manner indicated below:

11) Make the Latin noun **deus** plural, keeping the case the same.
12) Make the Latin noun **rem** plural, keeping the case the same.
13) Make the Latin noun **iter** plural, keeping the case the same.
14) Make the Latin verb **volebant** present tense, keeping the person the same.
15) Make the Latin verb **fuerant** imperfect tense, keeping the person the same.

(15 marks)

* **Contextus Fabulae**– This mythical story is told (using the Greek counterparts to the Roman deities in the story above) by the Greek epic poet Homer in his *Iliad* (Book 15 Lines 187-193). Try to find answers to the following questions yourself: What story does the Iliad tell? Who is the famous Trojan hero who dies in it? Who is the famous Greek hero whose death occurs shortly after the events that the Iliad closes with?

(If you find that research interesting, consider reading the Iliad in translation in full if you have not already done so – along with the Odyssey, it is one of the world's greatest pieces of literature!)

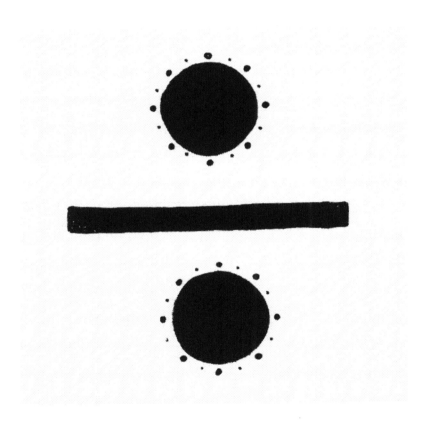

8. URANUS, GAIA AND CRONUS

The primal deity Uranus who, to the Greeks and Romans, was a personification of the sky (known as "Father Sky"), mates with Gaia ("Mother Earth"). However, he is then overthrown by one of his own sons, setting a chain of divine events in motion...

olim, antequam <u>Iuppiter</u> et <u>Iuno</u> (et ceteri illorum deorum qui domus in monte <u>Olympo</u> habebant) nati erant, <u>Uranus</u> nocte <u>Gaiae</u> concumbere solebat. mox igitur plurimi liberi nati sunt. hi liberi tamen Urano <u>odio erant</u>, quod monstra pessima - <u>Gigantes</u> <u>Cyclopes</u>que, nomine <u>Titanes</u> - erant. itaque ille eos in Tartarum inicere constituit. Gaia, cum cognovisset liberos suos in Tartaro iacere, tam misera erat ut consilium caperet: minimum filium, nomine Cronum, qui nondum in Tartarum iniectus est, rogavit ut patrem Uranum castraret.

Cronus, cum ambitiosus esset, matri paruit et ipse rex deorum factus est. Titanes autem e Tartaro non liberavit. itaque Gaia et Uranus <u>dixerunt</u> filium Croni quoque patrem <u>superaturum esse</u>. his verbis auditis, Cronus statim liberos suos consumere constituit. sed illa alia fabula est...

Iuppiter, Iovis, m – The God Jupiter (Greek name Zeus)
Iuno, Iunonis, f – The Goddess Juno (Greek name Hera)
Olympus, Olympi, m - Olympus
Uranus, Urani, m – Uranus ("Father Sky" – a primal deity)
Gaia, Gaiae, f – Gaia ("Mother Earth" – a primal deity)
odio erant – "were a source of hatred" (this use of the dative case is called the predicative dative)
Gigantes, Gigantum, m pl - giants
Cyclops, Cyclopis, m – a Cyclops
Titan, Titanis, m – a Titan

dixerunt – (here means) "(they) decreed", "they declared"

superaturum esse = "would overpower" (this is a future active infinitive)

From the story of Uranus, Gaia and Cronus above, answer the following questions relating to types of clauses found in the Latin:

1) Identify and write down a relative clause.
2) Identify and write down an ablative absolute.
3) Identify and write down a cum clause (i.e. a temporal clause using the subjunctive).
4) Explain why **caperet** is in the subjunctive mood.
5) Explain why **castraret** is in the subjunctive mood.

From the story of Uranus, Gaia and Cronus above, identify and write down in Latin one example of each of the following parts of speech:

6) A noun in the dative case.
7) A noun that is neuter and plural.
8) A present active infinitive.
9) A superlative form from the Latin adjective **malus, a, um**
10) A deponent verb.

Change the following words from the above story in the manner indicated below:

11) Make the Latin noun **matri** plural, keeping the case the same.
12) Make the Latin noun **monstra** singular, keeping the case the same.
13) Make the Latin verb **liberavit** pluperfect tense, keeping the person the same.
14) Write down the 1st person singular present tense of the Latin verb **habebant**.
15) Write down the 1st person singular present tense of the Latin verb **dixerunt**.

(15 marks)

* Contextus Fabulae– Part of the story above refers to punishments given to the race of Titans. Can you think of any individual Titans who received personal punishments of their own? (Hint to get you started – one such Titan is thought to have a mountain range named after him...)

GCSE STORIES

1. CEPHALUS AND PROCRIS

A tragic love story caused by misunderstanding and the jealousy of a goddess.

Cephalus iuvenis pulcher erat qui venationem amabat. Aurora, dea primae lucis, eum conspexit et statim amore incensa est. Cephalus tamen uxorem pulchram, nomine Procridem, habebat et eam magnopere amabat. Procris amica Dianae, deae venationis, erat; cui Diana canem celerrimum et hastam subtilimam dederat. invicem Procris haec dona Cephalo dedit.

mox Aurora intellexit Cephalum se non amare. itaque, irata, Cephalum dimisit his verbis dictis, "discede! sed tu, cum uxore mortale, miserrimus erit!"

Cephalus ad uxorem rediit et, verba deae neglegens, laetissimus erat. olim, fessus post venationem, in herbis prope flumen iacuit. "veni, vente placide, et me deleni!" magna voce dixit. deinde aliquis qui per eandem silvam ambulabat, cum haec verba audivisset, credidit Cephalum ad puellam adlocutum esse. ille igitur Procridem certiorem facere constituit. Procris miserrime lacrimabat, sed sine mora verum in hac re petere constituit.

proximo die igitur in silvas Cephalum secuta est et, cum ille requiesceret, se celavit. Cephalus iterum ad ventum placidum, "veni ad me!" clamavit. tum sonitum in virgultis audivit et, quod feram adesse credebat, hastam claram in virgulta iniecit; quae statim Procridem vulneravit. illa, paene mortua et veri nescia, Cephalum oravit ne amaret puellam cui dixisset. itaque Cephalus

miserrimus, re uxori explicata, se occidit.

Cephalus, Cephali, m – Cephalus (a person)
Aurora, Aurorae, f – The Goddess Aurora (Goddess of the Dawn, Greek name Eos)
Procris, Procridis, f – Procris (a person)
Diana, Dianae, f – The Goddess Diana (Greek name Artemis)
nescius, nescia, nescium + genitive – "ignorant of"

Copy out the table below in your exercise book:
In your second column give **one English word which comes from the Latin word** in the first column.
In your third column give the **meaning of your chosen English word**.
An example has been done for you.

Latin word	English word	Meaning of the English word
voce	vocal	relating to the voice
verbis		
flumen		
incensa est		
proximo		
audivit		

(10 marks)

2. ATALANTA

Atalanta is beaten at her own game by a clever trick!

Atalanta pulchra puella Graeca, filia regis Arcadiae, erat. multi viri eam amabant et in matrimonium ducere cupiebant. illa tamen viros non amabat. olim igitur consilium cepit: omnes viri, qui Atalantam amabant, ad cenam splendidam invitati sunt. mox, cum multum vinum bibissent, puella surrexit et haec verba dixit, "o viri, ego celerimme currere possum. si me in matrimonium ducere cupitis, contra me currite! me superate! sed cavete: omnes a me superati postea occidentur"

Hippomenes iuvenis pulcherrimus erat. simulatque ille Atalantam currentem conspexit, eam adeo amabat ut maritus eius esse magnopere cuperet. vir igitur, quamquam multi amicorum iam ab Atalanta occisi erant, contra puellam currere constituit.

ille ad templum Veneris, deae amoris, cucurrit et deam rogavit ut auxilium sibi daret. Venus tria poma aurea ei dedit. "haec cape", inquit, "et consilium, quod nunc tibi dabo, audi!" verbis deae auditis, Hippomenes celeriter discessit ut ad Atalantam rediret. "contra te curram", inquit.

Atalanta, quod celerius currere poterat, iuvenem superabat. itaque Hippomenes

unum pomorum ad terram deiecit. Atalanta constitit ut pomum caperet (quod

omnes puellae aurum amant). Hippomenes eam consecutus est. mox tamen

Atalanta illum iterum superabat. tum Hippomenes secundum pomum deiecit, et

iterum Atalanta constitit ut id tolleret. nunc Hippomenes prope Atalantam erat et

tertium pomum deiecit. cum Atalanta constiteret, Hippomenes denique puellam

superavit. "ego victor sum", clamavit, "tu uxor mea eris". "ita vero", Atalanta

ridens respondit, "sed ego te superavi quod et maritum et tria aurea poma

habeo!"

Atalanta, Atalantae, f – Atalanta (a person)
Arcadia, Arcadiae, f - Arcadia (a place)
in matrimonium duco, ducere, duxi, ductum = I marry (someone)
consilium capio, capere, cepi, captum = I make a plan, I come up with a plan
Hippomenes, Hippomenae, m – Hippomenes (a person)
Venus, Veneris, f – The Goddess Venus (Greek name Aphrodite)
consequor, consequi, consecutus sum – (here means) "I catch up to"

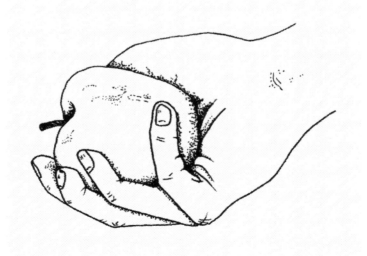

Answer the following questions about the story of Atalanta:

1) Who was Atalanta? (5)

2) Describe the feelings many men had towards her. (3)

3) To what were Atalanta's admirers invited? (2)

4) What must these admirers do if they want to marry her? (3)

5) What does Atalanta say will happen to those who try but fail to do this? (2)

6) Who was Hippomenes? (2)

7) What did he decide to do? (2)

8) What did he ask the Goddess Venus to do? (3)

9) Describe the actions taken by both Hippomenes and Atalanta which result in Hippomenes beating her in the race. (4)

10) Why does Atalanta claim to Hippomenes she has still come out on top, even though she has lost the race? (4)

(30 marks)

3. ECHO AND NARCISSUS

A story in which vanity is punished by a goddess in an appropriate fashion.

Echo nympha silvarum erat quae semper dicebat et cantabat et ridebat. olim Iuppiter, cum pulcherrimis nymphis montium concumbere cuperet, iussit Echum Iunonem avocare. Echo regi deorum paruit et fabulas longas Iunoni narravit. postea, ubi Iuno dolum Echus invenit, iratissima erat et exclamavit, "tace! nunc solum dices ea quae tibi dicuntur." Echo, ut deae responderet, os aperuit, sed nulla verba exierunt. "discede!", Iuno dixit. "discede...discede", Echo molliter respondit.

itaque illa, perterrita et misera, per silvas errabat. nunc nemo amicus eius esse cupiebat. uno die Echo Narcissum, puerum pulchrum, conspexit et statim amavit. cotidie, ad iuvenem spectandum, eum sequebatur. ille nympham saepe vidit sed ei non appropinquavit, quod superbus et gloriosus erat. tandem iratus fiebat quod Echo semper aderat. "abi!" clamavit, "ego non te amo!" "te amo...te amo", Echo respondit et, tristis, discessit; postea cibum non consumpsit et denique periit. vox tamen mansit. Narcissus, quamquam solam vocem in silvis audiebat, etiam non intellegebat nympham ipsam non iam adesse.

dea Diana, propter vanitatem et crudelitatem, iuvenem punire constituit. Narcissus, cum olim post venationem solus et fessus esset, prope lacunam sedit.

in aqua vultum suum conspexit et statim se amavit. cotidie in lacuna se spectabat et imaginem orabat ut ad se adveniret, sed frustra: imago, immobilis, nihil locuta est. tandem Narcissus, quod diu e lacuna non moverat, fame periit. ex illo tempore prope corpus flos quidam, nunc nomine Narcissus, crescebat.

Echo, Echus, f – Echo (a nymph)
Iuppiter, Iovis, m – The God Jupiter (Greek name Zeus)
Iuno, Iunonis, f – The Goddess Juno (Greek name Hera)
Narcissus, Narcissi, m – Narcissus (a person)
Diana, Dianae, f – The Goddess Diana (Greek name Artemis)
vanitas, vanitatis, f – (here means) "vanity", "conceit"

For each of the following excerpts from the Latin story of Echo and Narcissus, **choose which one statement is true**, and then **answer the comprehension question** which follows:

1) *ille nympham saepe vidit sed ei non appropinquavit...*

We are told here that ...

a) Narcissus always saw the nymph.
b) Narcissus often saw the nymph.
c) Narcissus always conquered the nymph.
d) Narcissus often conquered the nymph.

(1)

What are we told in this sentence that Narcissus did not do? (2)

2) *tandem iratus fiebat quod Echo semper aderat.*

We are told here that...

a) However, Narcissus was becoming angry.
b) However, Narcissus was becoming irritated.
c) At last Narcissus was becoming irritated.
d) At last Narcissus was becoming angry.

(1)

What is the reason given for this? (2)

3) *Narcissus, cum olim post venationem solus et fessus esset, prope lacunam sedit.*

We are told here that...

a) Narcissus stood near the lake.
b) Narcissus sat near the lake.
c) Narcissus stood in front of the lake.
d) Narcissus sat in front of the lake.

(1)

Describe in full how Narcissus is described in this sentence. (3)

(10 marks)

4. CERES AND PROSERPINA

The seasons of the year come into being as a result of a mother's pain at her daughter's absence…

Ceres, dea frumentorum, filiam nomine Proserpinam habebat. olim illa a matre erraverat ut flores carperet. subito Pluto, rex mortuorum in terra inferiore, ascendit in curru, et puellam conspectam rapuit. ad regnum suum Proserpinam perterritam abstulit ut eam in matrimonium duceret.

interea Ceres, quae diu frustra exclamabat, filiam invenire non poterat. tam tristis fiebat ut nihil in terra cresceret (cum dea misera nunc nec flores nec frumenta curaret). Iuppiter, qui omnia vidit, Mercurio, nuntio deorum, imperavit ut ex Orco ad terram vivorum Proserpinam reduceret. Pluto tamen uxorem liberare nolebat; "fas est", inquit, "si Proserpina cibum in Orco consumpsit, ei semper hic manere necesse erit."

Proserpina dixit, "solum sex semina mali Punici consumpsi". his verbis auditis, Pluto Mercurio dixit, "ea igitur sex anni menses hic manebit et sex menses in terra vivorum habitabit. Mercurius adnuit et, manum Proserpinae tenens, ex Orco eam ad matrem reduxit.

Ceres hos sex menses tam laeta erat ut omnia frumenta iterum crescerent. haec pars anni ab hominibus "ver et aestas" appellatur. ubi autem Proserpinae ad

Orcum redire necesse erat, Ceres iterum tristis erat et frumenta non iam

crescebant. haec pars anni tempus autumnale et hibernum est.

Ceres, Cereris, f – The Goddess Ceres (Greek name Demeter)
Proserpina, Proserpinae, f – The Goddess Proserpina (Greek name Persephone)
Pluto, Plutonis, m – The God Pluto (Greek name Hades)
in matrimonium duco, ducere, duxi, ductum – I marry (someone)
Iuppiter, Iovis, m – The God Jupiter (Greek name Zeus)
Mercurius, Mercurii, m – The God Mercury (Greek name Hermes)
Orcus, Orci, m – Orcus (a name for the Underworld)
fas – an indeclinable noun meaning "divine law"
malum Punicum, mali Punici, n – a pomegranate

<u>Answer the following questions about the story of Ceres and Proserpina:</u>

1) Who was Ceres? (1)

2) What did Pluto do after rising up from the Underworld in his chariot? (3)

3) Where did he then take Proserpina? (2)

4) What was his purpose in taking her there? (1)

5) What happened as a result of Ceres being sad when she could not find her daughter? (3)

6) What did Jupiter order Mercury to do? (4)

7) Having done what would result in Proserpina having to stay in the Underworld according to Pluto? (3)

8) Explain how much time Proserpina must now spend at a time and where she must spend it. (4)

9) What are the seasons of the year called when Proserpina is with her mother? (2)

10) What are the seasons of the year called when Proserpina is with Pluto? (2)

(25 marks)

5. BACCHUS, SEMELE, AND ARIADNE

Juno's jealousy at one of her husband's mortal lovers brings tragic results,

although Venus engineers a happy ending of sorts…

Bacchus filius Iovis et feminae mortalis nomine Semelae erat. Iuno irata

consilium cepit ut Semelam deleret. mutata veste, ad Semelam advenit et negavit

Iovem patrem Bacchi esse. Semela igitur curiosa erat et ab Iove gratiam petivit.

"promitto me tibi gratiam facturum esse", ille statim respondit. his verbis auditis,

Semela celeriter dixit, "splendorem caelestem gerentem te mihi ostende!"

"haec verba non mihi placet", Iuppiter inquit, "sed ea renuntiari nunc non

possunt." sua gloria divina fulgens, cubiculum Semelae intravit sed, quod corpus

mortale calorem dei ferre non poterat, illa in cineres incensa est.

post mortem matris, infans Bacchus a nymphis in silvis curabatur et cultum vitis

invenit. iuvenis multa itinera per Asiam Graeciamque fecit ut homines doceret

quomodo vinum faceretur. multos discipulos colligebat, et viros et feminas, qui

secum in ritibus ebriis, nomine Bacchanaliis, saltabant.

olim Bacchus, in insula Dia dormiens, a nautis captus est. illi in Aegypto eum

servum vendere cupiebant, sed subito navis in mari destitit. nautae eam movere

non poterant. vites ubique in nave crescebant et Bacchus ab animalibus sacris

suis - pantheris et lyncibus et tigribus - circumventus est. nautae perterriti in

mare se iecerunt et in delphinos mutati sunt.

deinde Bacchus ad insulam Diam rediit. haec erat insula ubi Ariadna, filia regis

Minois, a Theseo relicta erat. Venus tamen eam promiserat amatorem

immortalem habituram esse. itaque illa sedens et lacrimans a Baccho inventa est.

eam in matrimonium duxit et ei coronam gemmarum dedit. cum denique Ariadna

mortua esset, Bacchus hanc coronam in caelum iecit et statim gemmae in stellas

mutatae sunt.

Bacchus, Bacchi, m – The God Bacchus (Greek name Dionysus)
Iuppiter, Iovis, m – The God Jupiter (Greek name Zeus)
Semela, Semelae, f – Semele (a person)
Iuno, Iunonis, f – The Goddess Juno (Greek name Hera)
consilium capio, capere, cepi, captum – I come up with a plan
gratiam peto, petere, petivi, petitum – I ask for a favour
gratiam facio, facere, feci, factum – I grant a favour
cultus vitis, cultus vitis, m – "the tending of grapes"
Asia, Asiae, f – Asia
Graecia, Graeciae, f – Greece
Bacchanalia, Bacchanalium, n pl – The Bacchanalia (sacred rites of Bacchus)
Dia, Diae, f – Naxos (an island)
Aegyptus, Aegypti, f – Egypt
Ariadna, Ariadnae, f – Ariadne (a person)
Minos, Minois, m – Minos (a person)
Theseus, Thesei, m – Theseus (a person)
Venus, Veneris, f – The Goddess Venus (Greek name Aphrodite)
in matrimonium duco, ducere, duxi, ductum – I marry (someone)

Copy out the table below into your exercise book:

In your second column give **one English word which comes from the Latin word** in the first column.

In your third column give the **meaning of your chosen English word**.

An example has been done for you.

Latin word	English word	Meaning of the English word
corpus	corpse	dead body
feminae		
deleret		
intravit		
iuvenis		
sedens		

(10 marks)

6. PHAETHON AND THE CHARIOT OF THE SUN

Phaethon, son of Apollo, asks his father for proof of his divine birth…

olim Phaethon, filius Apollinis dei solis, iter fecit ut patrem suum in caelo videret. cum ille advenisset, statim sic patrem oravit, "si tibi placet, pater, da mihi signum, quod demonstrat me filium tuum esse. pueri in ludo rident quod non credunt te patrem meum esse."

"mi fili, scilicet tibi hanc gratiam faciam," respondit Apollo. "currum solis unum diem trans caelum pellere cupio," Phaethon inquit. Apollo tamen timebat ne filius occideretur. eum oravit ut haec reputaret, "illud non tutum est. equi validissimi sunt." sed pater filio persuadere non poterat.

currus solis aureus tam clarus erat ut Phaethon eum vix spectare posset. a quattuor ingentibus equis trahebatur.

mox sol oriebatur. Apollo ultima verba filio locutus est, "noli equos verberare quod sponte celerrime ibunt! noli currum pellere aut ad alteriorem aut inferiorem partem caeli, sed mane in media via." tandem stellae non iam effulgebant et prima luce Aurora purpureas portas orientales aperuit. deinde equi in caelum ruerunt, sed Phaethon iam eis imperare non poterat. currus altius ascendit et terra glacialis fiebat. tum currus inferius descendit et terra incendebatur: totae gentes perierunt et magnae urbes deletae sunt. flumina et

maria exaruerunt.

Dea Terrae Iovi clamavit, "rex deorum, me et fratrem meum Oceanum serva!

cur hanc fortunam accipere debemus?" his verbis auditis, Iuppiter omnes deos

convocavit ut rem spectarent. fulmen suum ad currum iacere constituit;

Phaethon crinibus incensis ad terram cecidit et periit.

Phaethon, Phaethontis, m – Phaethon (a person)
Apollo, Apollonis, m – The God Apollo (Greek name also Apollo)
gratiam facio, facere, feci, factum – I grant a favour
Aurora, Aurorae, f – The Goddess of the Dawn (Greek name Eos)
Dea Terrae, Deae Terrae, f – The Goddess Mother Earth (Greek name Gaia)
Iuppiter, Iovis, m – The God Jupiter (Greek name Zeus)
Oceanus, Oceani, m – The God Ocean (Greek name also Oceanus)

For each of the following excerpts from the Latin story of Phaethon and the chariot of the Sun, **choose which one statement is true**, and then **answer the comprehension question** which follows:

1) *…equi validissimi sunt." sed pater filio persuadere non poterat.*

We are told here that …

a) The father was able to persuade his son.
b) The father was unable to persuade his son.
c) The son was unable to persuade his father.
d) The son was able to persuade his father.

(1)

How are the horses described here? (2)

2) *deinde equi in caelum ruerunt, sed Phaethon iam eis imperare non poterat.*

The most accurate summary of what we are told in the second half of this sentence is that…

a) Phaethon was now unable to master the horses.
b) The horses were now unable to master Phaethon.
c) Phaethon was now able to master the horses.
d) The horses were now able to master Phaethon.

(1)

Where are the horses said to be rushing? (2)

3) *"rex deorum, me et fratrem meum <u>Oceanum</u> serva! cur hanc fortunam*

accipere debemus?"

We are told here that…

a) Mother Earth shouts to Jupiter to save her and her brother, Ocean.
b) Mother Earth shouts to Jupiter to save her and her father, Ocean.
c) Mother Earths shouts to Jupiter to enslave her and her brother, Ocean.
d) Mother Earth shouts to Jupiter to enslave her and her father, Ocean.

(1)

What question does Mother Earth ask Jupiter here? (3)

(10 marks)

Vocabulary for Level 2 Stories:

adfigo, adfigere, adfixi, adfixum - I fix (something) on

ala, alae, f - wing

alius, alia, aliud - other

amans, amantis, m/f - lover

amica, amicae, f - girlfriend, female friend

amor, amoris, m - love

anguis, anguis, m/f - a snake

angustiae, angustiarum, f pl - a strait (of water)

aperio, aperire, aperui, apertum - I open

apis, apis, f - a bee

arca, arcae, f - box, chest

ascendo, ascendere, ascendi, ascensum - I climb up

asilus, asili, m - gadfly

aut...aut...- either...or...

avis, avis, f - a bird

cado, cadere, cecidi, casum - I fall

caleo, calere, calui - I am hot

callidus, callida, callidum - clever

canis, canis, m - dog

cano, canere, cecini - I play (a musical instrument)

caput, capitis, n - head

carcer, carceris, n - prison

cauda, caudae, f - tail

celo, celare, celavi, celatum - I hide (something)

centum - a hundred

cera, cerae, f - wax

claudo, claudere, clausi, clausum - I close, I shut

consilium, consilii, n - a plan

consto, constare, constiti, constatum - I stand still, I come to a standstill

convenio, convenire, conveni, conventum - I meet, I come together

cotidie - everyday

credo, credere, credidi, creditum + dative - I trust, I believe

custodio, custodire, custodivi, custoditum - I guard

custos, custodis, m/f - a guard

decido, decidere, decidi - I fall down

deficio, deficere, defeci, defectum - I fail, I droop, I grow weak

deicio, deicere, deieci, deiectum - I throw down

dens, dentis, m - tooth

descendo, descendere, descendi, descensum - I go down, I climb down

dilanio, dilaniare, dilaniavi, dilaniatum - I tear to shreds

dissilio, dissilire, dissilui - I spring apart, I burst apart
dissolvo, dissolvere, dissolvi, dissolutum - I break (something) up
divido, dividere, divisi, divisum - I keep apart, I separate
dolus, doli, m - trick, deception
domina, dominae, f - mistress
dum - while, until
evanesco, evanescere, evanui - I vanish, I disappear
exclamo, exclamare, exclamavi, exclamatum - I cry out
exterior, exterius - outer, exterior (a comparative adjective)
fames, famis, f - hunger
fenestra, fenestrae, f - window
fera, ferae, f - a wild animal, a wild beast
ferox, ferocis - fierce
fidelis, fidele - loyal, trusty
fio, fieri, factus sum - I become
fleo, flere, flevi, fletum - I weep
fortasse - perhaps
frigidus, frigida, frigidum - cold (used of weather or of temperament)
gemma, gemmae, f - jewel
gemo, gemere, gemui, gemitum - I groan
ignis, ignis, m - fire
imago, imaginis, f - image, vision, ghost, spectre
includo, includere, inclusi, inclusum - I shut in
ingeniosus, ingeniosa, ingeniosum - gifted with genius, talented
inicio, inicere, inieci, iniectum - I throw (something) in
inquit - he/she says, he/she said
intellego, intellegere, intellexi, intellectum - I realise, I understand
inventor, inventoris, m - inventor
lacero, lacerare, laceravi, laceratum - I tear to pieces
lacuna, lacunae, f - lake, pool
lavo, lavare, lavi, lautum - I wash
leo, leonis, m - lion
libertas, libertatis, f - freedom
litus, litoris, n - shore, coast
lucerna, lucernae, f - a lamp
lyra, lyrae, f - a lyre (a musical instrument)
maritus, mariti, m - husband
mensis, mensis, m - month
monstrum, monstri, n - monster
morbus, morbi, m - sickness, disease
mordeo, mordere, momordi, morsum - I bite
mortalis, mortale - mortal, subject to death

muto, mutare, mutavi, mutatum - I change

nato, natare, natavi, natatum - I swim

neque...neque... - neither...nor...

nidus, nidi, m - nest, hive

nudus, nuda, nudum - naked

nympha, nymphae, f - a nymph

oblino, oblinere, oblevi, oblitum - I besmear, I dirty (something)

obtineo, obtinere, obtinui, obtentum - I hold in check

oculus, oculi, m - eye

oro, orare, oravi, oratum - I beg (someone for something - this verb is followed by 2 accusatives)

os, oris, n - mouth

pavo, pavonis, m - peacock

pectus, pectoris, n - chest, breast

penna, pennae, f - feather

permitto, permittere, permisi, permissum + dative + infinitive - I allow (someone to do something)

persuadeo, persuadere, persuasi, persuasum + dative - I persuade

pes, pedis, m - foot

peto, petere, petivi, petitum - I seek, I go to fetch

placeo, placere, placui, placitum - I please

relinquo, relinquere, reliqui, relictum - I leave behind

respicio, respicere, respexi, respectum - I look back

rima, rimae, f - a crack

rubeo, rubere, rubui - I blush

sanguis, sanguinis, m - blood

sacerdos, sacerdotis, f - priestess

satyrus, satyri, m - a satyr (a hairy wood deity)

sculptor, sculptoris, m - a sculptor

si - if

silva, silvae, f - forest, wood

sol, solis, m - the sun

soleo, solere, solitus - I am accustomed

solium, solii, n - seat, throne

statua, statuae, f - a statue

superbus, superba, superbum - arrogant, proud

supersum, superesse, superfui - I am left over, I am the remainder

suspiciosus, suspiciosa, suspiciosum - suspicious

tango, tangere, tetigi, tactum - I touch

taurus, tauri, m - bull

tempestas, tempestatis, f - storm

terribilis, terribile - dreadful

transfigo, transfigere, transfixi, transfixum - I pierce through
turris, turris, f - a tower
vacca, vaccae, f - cow
velamen, velaminis, n - veil
venatrix, venatricis, f - huntress
veto, vetare, vetui, vetitum - I forbid
vicinus, vicini, m - neighbour
villa, villae, f - house
violenter - violently
virgo, virginis, f - maiden
visito, visitare, visitavi, visitatum - I visit
volo, volare, volavi, volatum - I fly

Vocabulary for Level 3 Stories:

adroganter - arrogantly
ago, agere, egi, actum - I do, I carry out
ala, alae, f - a wing
alius, alia, aliud - other
amor, amoris, m - love
anxius, anxia, anxium - anxious, concerned
appareo, apparere, apparui, apparitum - I appear, I come into sight
appello, appellare, appellavi, appellatum - I call (someone or something a name)
aquila, aquilae, f - an eagle
aranea, araneae, f - spider
arbor, arboris, f - tree
ars, artis, f - art, craft, skill
ascendo, ascendere, ascendi, ascensum - I climb up
asilus, asili, m - a gadfly
aureus, aurea, aureum - golden, made of gold
bracchium, bracchii, n - an arm
caecus, caeca, caecum - blind
caper, capri, m - a goat
caput, capitis, n - head
carbo, carbonis, m - a piece of burning wood, some embers
carmen, carminis, n - poem, song
casa, casae, f - hut, cottage
cauda, caudae, f - a tail
celo, celare, celavi, celatum - I hide (something)
cena, cenae, f - dinner
certamen, certaminis, n - a contest
circumspicio, circumspicere, circumspexi, circumspectum - I look around
cognosco, cognoscere, cognovi, cognitum - I realise, I recognise, I get to know
corripio, corripere, corripui, correptum - I snatch away quickly
cotidie - every day
creo, creare, creavi, creatum - I create
crinis, crinis, m - hair
crudus, cruda, crudum - raw, uncooked
crus, cruris, n - leg
culpa, culpae, f - fault, blame
curo, curare, curavi, curatum - I take care of, I look after
decerno, decernere, decrevi, decretum - I determine, I perceive
denique - finally
deripio, deripere, deripui, dereptum - I tear away
descendo, descendere, descendi, descensum - I go down, I climb down

devolo, devolare, devolavi, devolatum - I fly down
dissimilis, dissimile + dative - unlike
dives, divitis - rich
dulcis, dulce - sweet, pleasant
effundo, effundere, effudi, effusum - I pour out
epistula, epistulae, f - a letter
equito, equitare, equitavi, equitatum - I ride
exclamo, exclamare, exclamavi, exclamatum - I cry out
exhalo, exhalare, exhalavi, exhalatum - I breathe out
exsurgo, exsurgere, exsurrexi, exsurrectum - I rise up, I rear up
falso (adverb) - by mistake, wrongly
fera, ferae, f - a wild beast, a wild animal
finio, finire, finivi, finitum - I finish
fio, fieri, factus sum - I become
flos, floris, m - a flower
formo, formare, formavi, formatum - I mould, I shape
frenum, freni, n - a bridle
frigidus, frigida, frigidum - cold (used of weather or of temperament)
frons, frondis, f - a leaf
gravis, grave - heavy
horresco, horrescere, horrui - I bristle up
hospes, hospitis, m - guest
hospitium, hospitii, n - friendship, hospitality
humanus, humana, humanum - human
iacto, iactare, iactavi, iactatum - I fling violently
iecur, iecoris, n - liver
ignis, ignis, m - fire
ignosco, ignoscere, ignovi, ignotum + dative - I forgive
immitto, immittere, immisi, immissum - I send (something) at, I let (something) loose on
impono, imponere, imposui, impositum - I set something in(to)/on(to)
incendo, incendere, incendi, incensum - I set on fire
inhibeo, inhibere, inhibui, inhibitum - I restrain, I check
inicio, inicere, inieci, iniectum - I thrown (something) in
inquit - he/she says, he/she said
inspiro, inspirare, inspiravi, inspiratum + dative - I blow on
intellego, intellegere, intellexi, intellectum - I realise, I understand
invideo, invidere, invidi, invisum + dative - I envy
ita vero - yes, indeed so
laurus, lauri, f - a laurel tree
lavo, lavare, lavi, lautum - I wash
leo, leonis, m - a lion

libenter - willingly, gladly

litus, litoris, n - shore, coast

ludi, ludorum, m pl - (public) games

lugeo, lugere, luxi, luctum - I mourn for, I grieve over

lutum, luti, n - clay, mud

membrum, membri, n - a limb

mensa, mensae, f - table

mollis, molle - soft, gentle

monstrum, monstri, n - a monster

mordeo, mordere, momordi, morsum - I bite

muto, mutare, mutavi, mutatum - I change

nato, natare, natavi, natatum - I swim

natura, naturae, f - nature, disposition

niger, nigra, nigrum - black

nympha, nymphae, f - a nymph

odor, odoris, m - smell

oro, orare, oravi, oratum - I beg

os, oris, n - face

ovis, ovis, f - sheep

paene - nearly, almost

pareo, parere, parui, paritum + dative - I obey

pastor, pastoris, m - shepherd

pectus, pectoris, n - chest, breast

pendeo, pendere, pependi - I hang

percutio, percutere, percussi, percussum - I strike

periculosus, periculosa, periculosum - dangerous

permitto, permittere, permisi, permissum + dative + infinitive - I allow (someone to do something)

pictura, picturae, f - (here means) a piece of embroidery

pluma, plumae, f - a feather

plumbeus, plumbea, plumbeum - made of lead

populus, populi, m - the people, the population

postridie - on the next day

potens, potentis - mighty, powerful

praemium, praemii, n - a prize

primo (adverb) - first, at first

quidam, quaedam, quoddam - a certain

ramus, rami, m - a branch

rapio, rapere, rapui, raptum - I snatch hold of

recresco, recrescere, recrevi, recretum - I grow again, I grow back

regia, regiae, f - palace

regnum, regni, n - kingdom

retineo, retinere, retinui, retentum - I retain
ripa, ripae, f - a river bank
rumpo, rumpere, rupi, ruptum - I break apart
saluto, salutare, salutavi, salutatum - I greet
sanguis, sanguinis, m - blood
saxum, saxi, n - a rock
scelestus, scelesta, scelestum - wicked, villainous
sedeo, sedere, sedi, sessum - I sit
sentio, sentire, sensi, sensum - I feel, I experience
serpens, serpentis, m/f - a snake
sidus, sideris, n - a constellation
silva, silvae, f - forest, wood
similis + dative - like, similar to
simul - at the same time
soleo, solere, solitus sum - I am accustomed
statua, statuae, f - a statue
stella, stellae, f - star
surripio, surripere, surripui, surreptum - I snatch away secretly
tam - so, such
tango, tangere, tetigi, tactum - I touch
tela, telae, f - a loom
tempus, temporis, n - time
texo, texere, texui, textum - I weave
textrix, textricis, f - a (female) weaver
textura, texturae, f - a piece of weaving
tollo, tollere, sustuli, sublatum - I lift up, I pick up
torpor, torporis, m - numbness, sluggishness
ubique - everywhere
unde - from where
ursa, ursae, f - a she-bear
uva, uvae, f - a grape
vasto, vastare, vastavi, vastatum - I lay waste to, I ravage
vates, vatis, m - a prophet, a soothsayer
venatio, venationis, f – hunting, the hunt
venatrix, venatricis, f - a huntress
victor, victoris, m - a victor, winner
villus, villi, m - shaggy hair, fleece
vincio, vincire, vinxi, vinctum - I tie up, I bind
visito, visitare, visitavi, visitatum - I visit
vito, vitare, vitavi, vitatum - I shun, I avoid
vivo, vivere, vixi, victum - I live
volo, volare, volavi, volatum - I fly

Vocabulary for 13+ Scholarship Stories:

accurro, accurrere, accurri, accursum – I run towards (something)

adfirmo, adfirmare, adfirmavi, adfirmatum - I declare

adnuo, adnuere, adnui, adnutum - I nod my agreement

aeternalis, aeternale - eternal

ago, agere, egi, actum - I carry out, I conduct, I set in motion

alius, alia, aliud - a different, another

amans, amantis, m/f - a lover

ambitiosus, ambitiosa, ambitiosum = ambitious, striving to advance oneself

amplexus, amplexus, m - an embrace

anima, animae, f - a soul

aper, apri, m - a wild boar

appello, appellare, appellavi, appellatum - I call (someone or something a name)

aquila, aquilae, f - an eagle

arbor, arboris, f - tree

arcus, arcus, m - a bow

aufero, auferre, abstuli, ablatus – I carry off

aureus, aurea, aureum - golden, made of gold

castro, castrare, castravi, castratum = I castrate (i.e. here: "I cut the testicles off")

certamen, certaminis, n – a contest

clam - in secret

claudus, clauda, claudum – lame, limping

cognosco, cognoscere, cognovi, cognitum – I get to know

compono, componere, composui, compositum – I organize, I bring together, I settle

concumbo, concumbere, concubui, concubitum + dative - I lie with, I have sex with

consilium, consilii, n - a plan

convivium, convivii, n – banquet, feast

convoco, convocare, convocavi, convocatum - I call together, I assemble

creo, creare, creavi, creatum - I create

currus, currus, m - a chariot

decerno, decernere, decrevi, decretum – I resolve, I settle (a question or debate)

denego, denegare, denegavi, denegatum - I say no, I flatly refuse

denique - finally

derideo, deridere, derisi, derisum - I mock, I deride

descendo, descendere, descendi, descensum - I go down, I climb down

designo, designare, designavi, designatum – I appoint, I set up

divido, dividere, divisi, divisum - I divide into parts

doceo, docere, docui, doctum (+ 2 accusatives for the person being taught and for what they are being taught) - I teach

dolus, doli, m - trickery, guile

dubium, dubii, n - doubt

emitto, emittere, emisi, emissum - I send out, I send forth

eripio, eripere, eripui, ereptum - I tear away by force, I snatch away

expello, expellere, expuli, expulsum - I drive out, I expel

exsulto, exsultare, exsultavi, exsultatum – I rejoice gleefully

fabula, fabulae, f - a story

fera, ferae, f - a wild animal, a wild beast

ferrum, ferri, n - iron

festum, festi, n - a festival

fingo, fingere, finxi, fictum - I arrange, I shape, I fashion

fio, fieri, factus sum – I become

fons, fontis, m – a spring (of water)

gaudeo, gaudere, gavisus sum - I rejoice (+ in + ablative for what is being rejoiced in)

gemini, geminorum, m pl - twins

iaceo, iacere, iacui – I lie (as in "lie down")

iampridem – a long time ago

immortalitas, immortalitatis, f – immortality

impono, imponere, imposui, impositum - I set something in(to)

improbus, improba, improbum - naughty, shameless

inicio, inicere, inieci, iniectum – I throw (someone or something) into

insidiae, insidiarum , f pl – A trap, snare (NB: this noun is plural in form but singular in meaning)

iudex, iudicis, m – a judge, arbitrator

iuste - fairly, justly

lacrimo, lacrimare, lacrimavi, lacrimatum - I cry

lateo, latere, latui – I lie hidden

lectus, lecti, m - a bed

lex, legis, f - law

liber, libera, liberum - free

liberi, liberorum, m pl - children

lingua, linguae, f - tongue

lupus, lupi, m - wolf

malo, malle, malui – I prefer, I am inclined towards something

materia, materiae, f – wood for building things, lumber

mollio, mollire, mollivi, mollitum - I soothe, I soften

monstrum, monstri, n - a monster

nascor, nasci, natus sum - I am born

nondum = not yet

nympha, nymphae, f - a nymph

obtineo, obtinere, obtinui, obtentum - I obtain, I get hold of oleum, olei, n - oil

orior, oriri, ortus sum – I rise up

ovis, ovis, f – a sheep

pareo, parere, parui, paritum + dative - I obey

patefacio, patefacere, patefeci, patefactum - I reveal, I disclose

paulatim - gradually, little by little

persequor, persequi, persecutus sum - I chase after, I hunt

peto, petere, petivi, petitum - I seek, I go after

pincerna, pincernae, m – a cupbearer (NB: masculine 1st declension noun)

placeo, placere, placui, placitum - I please

placidus, placida, placidum – calm, gentle, peaceful

prima aetas, primae aetatis, f – youth (literally "the first period of life")

primo (adverb) - first, at first

primum (adverb) - first, in the first place

promitto, promittere, promisi, promissum - I promise

pudor, pudoris, m - shame

pulso, pulsare, pulsavi, pulsatum - I strike

puto, putare, putavi, putatum - I think

quotannis – every year, annually

rabies, rabiei, f – madness, fervour

regia, regiae, f – palace

regnum, regni, n – a kingdom

rete, retis, n - a net, a snare

revenio, revenire, reveni, reventum - I return

revivisco, reviviscere, revivixi – I am restored to life, I come to life again

ripa, ripae, f - a river bank

ruber, rubra, rubrum - red, ruddy

saeculum, saeculi, n – age, generation

salsus, salsa, salsum - salty

sanguis, sanguinis, m - blood

sidus, sideris, n - a constellation

silva, silvae, f - forest, wood

soleo, solere, solitus sum (a semi-deponent verb) + infinitive – I am accustomed (to do something)

sors, sortis, f – a lot (i.e. an individual lot used when deciding something by lots)

sortior, sortiri, sortitus sum – I draw lots (i.e. a method of decision making)

spectaculum, spectaculi, n - a spectacle, a sight

stella, stellae, f - star

strepitus, strepitus, m - a din, a crashing sound

sustollo, sustollere, sustuli, sublatum - I take up, I lift up

talis, tale – such, of such a kind

totiens - so often, so many times

tridens, tridentis, m - trident
ulciscor, ulcisci, ultus sum - I take vengeance upon
ullus, ulla, ullum - any, any at all
ursus, ursi, m - a (male) bear
vehementer - violently
venator, venatoris, m - hunter
victrix, victricis, f - a (female) winner

Vocabulary for GCSE stories:

adloquor, adloqui, adlocutus sum - I speak to, I address
adnuo, adnuere, adnui, adnutum - I nod my approval, I nod my consent
advenio, advenire, adveni, adventum - I arrive
aestas, aestatis, f - summer
aliquis, aliquid – somebody, someone
amator, amatoris, m - lover
amica, amicae, f - friend, girlfriend
animal, animalis, n - animal
antequam - before
aperio, aperire, aperui, apertum - I open
appello, appellare, appellavi, appellatum - I call by name
ascendo, ascendere, ascendi, ascensum - I climb up
aureus, aurea, aureum - golden, made of gold
aurum, auri, n - gold
autumnalis, autumnale - autumnal, of autumn
avoco, avocare, avocavi, avocatum - I divert, I call away, I distract
bibo, bibere, bibi - I drink
cado, cadere, cecidi, casum - I fall down
caelestis, caelesti - of heaven
calor, caloris, m – heat, glow
canis, canis, m - dog
canto, cantare, cantavi, cantatum - I sing
carpo, carpere, carpsi, carptum - I pluck
celeriter - quickly
certeriorem facio, facere, feci, factum - I inform
cinis, cineris, m - ashes
circumvenio, circumvenire, circumveni, circumventum - I surround
clarus, clara, clarum - bright, clear, famous
colligo, colligere, collegi, collectum - I gather together, I collect
concumbo, concumbere, concubui, concubitum + dative - I sleep with
consto, constare, constiti, constatum - I come to a standstill
contra + accusative - against
convoco, convocare, convocavi, convocatum - I call together, I assemble
corona, coronae, f – crown, wreath
cotidie – every day
cresco, crescere, crevi, cretum - I grow
crinis, crinis, m - hair
crudelitas, crudelitatis, f - cruelty
cubiculum, cubiculi, n - bedroom
curiosus, curiosa, curiosum – curious, inquisitive

curo, curare, curavi, curatum - I care for, I look after
currus, currus, m - chariot
deicio, deicere, deieci, deiectum - I throw down
delenio, delenire, delenivi, delenitum - I soothe, I calm
delphinus, delphini, m - dolphin
demonstro, demonstrare, demonstravi, demonstratum - I demonstrate, I point out
denique - finally
descendo, descendere, descendi, descensum – I go down, I climb down
desisto, desistere, destiti, destitum - I stop
dimitto, dimittere, dimisi, dimissum - I send away, I dismiss
discipulus, discipuli, m - follower
divinus, divina, divinum - divine
dolus, doli, m - trickery, deception
ebrius, ebria, ebrium - drunken
effulgeo, effulgere, effulsi - I shine forth
erro, errare, erravi, erratum - I wander, I roam
exaresco, exarescere, exarui - I dry up completely
exclamo, exclamare, exclamavi, exclamatum - I cry out
exeo, exire, exi(v)i, exitum - I go out
explico, explicare, explicavi, explicatum - I explain
fabula, fabulae, f - story
fames, famis, f - hunger
fera, ferae, f - wild beast
fessus, fessa, fessum - tired
fio, fieri, factus sum - I become
flos, floris, m - flower
fortuna, fortunae, f - fortune, fate
frumentum, frumenti, n - grain, crop
fulgeo, fulgere, fulsi - I flash with light
fulmen, fulminis, n - thunderbolt
gemma, gemmae, f - jewel
gens, gentis, f - race, people, clan
gero, gerere, gessi, gestum - I wear, I bear
glacialis, glaciale - icy, frozen
gloria, gloriae, f - glory
gloriosus, gloriosa, gloriosum - arrogant, boasting
hasta, hastae, f - spear
herba, herbae, f - grass
hibernus, hiberna, hibernum - of winter, wintry
hic (indeclinable) - here
idem, eadem, idem - the same
imago, imaginis, f - image, reflection, ghost

immobilis, immobile - unmoving
immortalis, immortale - immortal
infans, infantis, m - little child
inferus, infera, inferum - below, lower, underneath
invicem - in turn
invito, invitare, invitavi, invitatum - I invite
ita vero - yes
lacuna, lacunae, f – lake, pool
loquor, loqui, locutus sum - I speak
ludus, ludi, m - school
lux, lucis, f - light
lynx, lyncis, m/f - a lynx
magnopere - greatly
mensis, mensis, m - month
molliter - softly
mora, morae, f - delay
morior, mori, mortuus sum - I die
mortalis, mortale - mortal
mortuus, mortua, mortuum - dead
moveo, movere, movi, motum - I move
muto, mutare, mutavi, mutatum - I change
ne + subjunctive - so that not
necesse (an indeclinable adjective) - necessary
neglego, neglegere, neglexi, neglectum - I ignore, I do not heed
nego, negare, negavi, negatum - I say that…not, I deny
nympha, nymphae, f - nymph
orientalis, orientale - of the East, Eastern
orior, oriri, ortus sum - I rise
os, oris, n - mouth
panthera, pantherae, f – a panther
pareo, parere, parui, paritum + dative - I obey
pello, pellere, pepuli, pulsum - I drive, push
placet (impersonal verb)- it is pleasing
placidus, placida, placidum - gentle, tranquil, calm
pomum, pomi, n - apple, piece of fruit
porta, portae, f - gate
punio, punire, punivi, punitum - I punish
purpureus, purpurea, purpureum – purple, purple-coloured
quidam, quaedam, quoddam - a certain
reduco, reducere, reduxi, reductum - I lead back
regnum, regni, n – kingdom, realm
renuntio, renuntiare, renuntiavi, renuntiatum - I take back, I renounce

reputo, reputare, reputavi, reputatum - I think over again
requiesco, requiescere, requievi, requietum - I rest
ritus, ritus, m - rite, religious ritual
ruo, ruere, rui, rutum - I rush
salto, saltare, saltavi, saltatum - I dance
scilicet - of course
semen, seminis, n - seed
sequor, sequi, secutus sum - I follow, I pursue
simulac, simulatque - as soon as
sol, solis, m - the sun
solum - only
sonitus, sonitus, m – sound, noise, din
specto, spectare, spectavi, spectatum - I look at, I watch
splendidus, splendida, splendidum - splendid
splendor, splendoris, m - splendour, brilliance, brightness
sponte - of (his/her/its/their) own accord
stella, stellae, f - star
subtilis, subtile - fine, slender, delicate
superbus, superba, superbum - proud
surgo, surgere, surrexi, surrectum - I get up
tigris, tigris, f - tiger
tollo, tollere, sustuli, sublatum - I lift up, I pick up
tutus, tuta, tutum - safe
ubique - everywhere
ultimus, ultima, ultimum - last
validus, valida, validum - strong
venatio, venationis, f – a hunt
vendo, vendere, vendidi, venditum - I sell
ventus, venti, m - wind
ver, veris, n – spring (the season)
verbero, verberare, verberavi, verberatum - I flog, I beat
verum, veri, n - the truth
vestis, vestis, f - clothing
victor, victoris, m - victor, winner
virgulta, virgultorum, n pl - thickets
vitis, vitis, f - grape, grapevine
vivus, viva, vivum - alive
vix - scarcely
vulnero, vulnerare, vulneravi, vulneratum - I wound